5715577

ROBERTS, S.
Bird-keeping and birdcages:
a history
£2.95

636·686

8112

Hertfordshire

D1612930

28. JUL. 1986
- 6 MAR 1987

L 33

BIRD-KEEPING
and
BIRDCAGES:
A History

The world's most expensive birdcage? Price tag £975 ($2,535)

BIRD-KEEPING
and
BIRDCAGES:
A History

Sonia Roberts

DAVID & CHARLES : NEWTON ABBOT

ISBN 0 7153 5598 8

COPYRIGHT NOTICE
© Sonia Roberts 1972
All rights reserved. No part of this publication
may be reproduced, stored in a retrieval
system, or transmitted, in any form
or by any means, electronic, mechanical,
photocopying, recording or otherwise,
without the prior permission of
David & Charles (Publishers) Limited

HERTFORDSHIRE
COUNTY LIBRARY

636.6860(

5715577

Set in 11/13pt Bembo
by C E Dawkins (Typesetters) Limited, London SE1
and printed in Great Britain
by Lowe & Brydone (Printers) Limited, London NW10
for David & Charles (Publishers) Limited
South Devon House Newton Abbot Devon

Contents

List of Illustrations

CHAPTER ONE
Ancient Times

The history of birdkeeping can be traced to the very dawn of civilisation. Indeed it is reasonable to claim that caged birds were man's first true pets for, although the dog and cat predate the cage bird as companions of man, they were originally co-opted as assistants in hunting and vermin control respectively.

In many cultures, apart from the sacred birds kept in temples, trained or tamed birds were maintained in royal menageries—perhaps to impress subjects by showing that the king could rule nature as well as nations— and seem to predate the keeping of birds for food, like chickens.

The brilliance of birds' plumage and the beauty of their song have been obvious attractions to man; so has the fascination of studying flight at close quarters. Until the twentieth century, of course, flight was confined to birds, balloons and the divine. Interestingly, bats, on the borderline between true sky-soaring flight and the mammalian gliding of creatures like the 'flying' fox or 'flying' squirrel, have been favourite subjects for supernatural associations and folklore. It is not only in simple societies such as those of aboriginal Australia or primitive Polynesia, or in the totem and tabu cultures of the North and South American Indians, that birds and birdlike figures play a vital role in religious myth. Among

Birdcage in Byzantine tiles

12

the winged deities of the world, the Semitic vision, reaching its sophisticated ultimate in the angels, seraphs and cherubs of the *Book of Revelations*, cannot be omitted. The Hebrew patriarchy numbered at least one knowledgeable fancier in Noah: the use of bird symbolism in the dramatic tale of the Great Flood implies that the early tellers of the tale and their listeners would be familiar with the habits of ravens and the homing instinct of doves.

Obviously, in the early history of aviculture, the dividing line between pets on the one hand, and domesticated birds reared for the table on the other, tended to be more blurred than it is today, though even now it would be difficult to decide on which side of the fence the pheasant should be placed. Imported stocks of pheasants were successfully released all over Western Europe and have established themselves as wildlings, which in some districts of southern England are close to being pests. Yet if the watchful eye of the gamekeeper were wholly withdrawn from this species it might not be sufficiently strong to survive, and in many areas, of course, it is still maintained wholly captive in pheasantries for sale as food or to be released solely for shooting.

What is clear is that birds kept as objects of curiosity and interest rather than purely to supply the table have been a commonplace since 1500 BC. This is the date when contemporary records reveal that Queen Hatshepsut of Egypt financed an expedition to the wildest regions of her kingdom and beyond, for the purpose of bringing back live specimens of exotic wildlife to adorn the royal zoo. Since the Egyptian pantheon contained a hawk-headed god, Horus, it is reasonable to suppose that falcons were revered in much the same way as the more famous temple cats and crocodiles of the old Nile regions. That pantheon also included ibis-headed supernaturals, while vultures and geese regularly appear on tomb murals both as sacred emblems and in scenes of everyday life.

Some antiquaries suggest that, along with gunpowder, printing, porcelain manufacture and numerous other civilised crafts, the Chinese invented aviculture, using selective breeding to fix the characteristics of certain classes of ornamental pheasant while Europe was still prehistoric.

Certainly there are written records of domesticated cormorants being employed in fishing by the Chinese from 600 BC.

Quail were favourite domesticated or pet birds in ancient times. A history of birdkeeping produced in the fourth century BC gives specific instructions on how to construct a quail pen, while the fact that the Greeks adorned their domestic pottery with illustrations of caged quails bears witness to their liking for these charming little birds. The British Museum in London has in its collection a drinking bowl of c480 BC which shows a youth releasing his pet quail from a knob-topped curved birdcage: from the outline of its shape the cage seems to have been made from either wicker or wood.

Alexander the Great took a keen interest in ornithology. When he reached India on his itinerary of conquest, he was enthralled by the beauty of the peacocks he saw there, and sent several specimens home. He also decreed that within the lands under his control—at one stage the greater part of the then known world—it would be a crime to slaughter peacock for the table. By Roman times, however, despite the fact that the peacock was the sacred emblem of the goddess Juno, consort of Jove himself, it frequently appeared as the centrepiece dish of a banquet, often stuffed with a variety of smaller birds set one within the other. The custom of serving roast peacock trimmed with its own splendid tail as a dish of honour was to remain part of the gastronomic tradition of Western Europe until well into the seventeenth century.

The geese that kept watch on the Capitol and, by their cackling at the approach of the Gaulish invaders, roused the guard to save Rome, are famous in legend. Many private citizens in Rome employed caged magpies to perform the same function at the entry porches of their houses. Magpies, which presumably amused their owners by reciting a few phrases of human speech, were regularly kept also as an entertainment for customers waiting their turn in Roman barbers' shops. The bones of caged ravens repeatedly turn up during the archaeological excavation of Roman townships, where it is extremely unlikely that they would have lived wild.

In the days of the empire, rich Romans frequently adorned their country-house gardens with aviaries. Visiting guests thought it worth noting in their memoirs that Lucullus, reportedly a gourmet host, was in the habit of letting pet birds flutter round his dining-rooms. An immensely rich speculative builder, Marcus Terentius Varro, one of the pioneers of mass-produced central heating systems for Roman cities, had a lavish aviary at his villa at Casinum: it consisted of three colonnaded chambers and a domed house containing several hundred birds of assorted species in porticoed bays and restrained by hemp nets rather than rigid bars. When the villa was excavated in the eighteenth century a clear floor-plan of the aviary was discovered; it is listed among the villa's amenities in R. Castell's *Villas of the Ancients*, first published in 1788.

Excursions into Africa had, early on, introduced the Romans to the charms of parrots as pets, and subsequently these accompanied their masters to all the outposts of the Empire, not excluding the British Isles, where once again the Roman love of sensible indoor temperatures, and their skill in maintaining them, must have been a boon in prolonging the lives of such exotic pets.

In encountering and conquering the Gauls, the Romans—whose legions themselves marched under eagle-topped standards—met a people who not only held the hawk sacred, but were themselves keen falconers.

Guinea fowl were also widely kept throughout the Roman Empire. The bones of what must have been a pet guinea fowl, with an elaborate metal leg-ring, were discovered during the excavation of a villa in Silchester, Hampshire, which at the time of its construction was on the edge of the Roman world. Yet within a few centuries guinea fowl had died out completely in the West and it was not until they were redis-covered by Portugese traders visiting Africa's Guinea coast in the fifteenth century (hence the name) that they were re-established in European avi-culture. They were again plentiful in France by the mid-sixteenth century, and were officially reintroduced into England in 1550. British naturalist George Edwards, born in 1694, wrote in 1760 that 'guinea fowl are now common domestic birds, whereas in my childhood they were rarities'

Aviculture is essentially a pursuit that demands a settled existence. Caged birds are cumbersome to move, and attempts to do so within the nesting season can severely limit, if not wholly inhibit, successful breeding. Thus the collapse of the Romans, and the break-up of the Empire's former Western provinces into tribal states, brought to an end the classical era of aviculture. However, as the Saxons, Franks, Jutes, Angles, Norsemen and Danes eventually established and settled territories far removed from their old homelands, so aviculture revived in the western world in two forms: the secular, based on keeping hawks for sport; and the monastic, in which chickens, ducks and, most of all, doves were 'factory farmed'.

Although the falconers of the Dark Ages were easily able to replenish their stocks from wild birds, breeding within the mews itself became a feature of the sport, and rivalry between birds of various regions, and even among birds from the 'stable' of a particularly skilled falconer, became intense. Thus one of St Boniface's major commissions when he left Britain to take up a mission in France in 750 was to acquire for his patron, King Ethelbert, 'two prime falcons trained to fly at cranes'.

An ability to perform expertly in the field of falconry was indeed almost compulsory for British sovereigns from the age of Alfred to that

Three hoods for hawks

of Elizabeth. Asser, in his life of Alfred, prizes his master's skill at hunting and falconry almost above his ability, remarkable for the age, to read and write.

In medieval London most of the area now given up to Trafalgar Square was a Royal Mews, founded by Richard III. During this period it was common to link falconry and dovekeeping by building a dovecote in the centre of the falconry court or mews, to supply prey for the falcons. Mews is, of course, one of the many phrases derived from the sport of falconry that has persisted into the present day. Although in modern parlance 'mews premises' tends to mean stables or, even more recently, garages, with living accommodation above, the mews was originally a home for hawks.

The Tudors' high regard for hawks can be gauged by the fact that the hawk emblem was awarded to Anne Boleyn on her ennoblement before her marriage to Henry VIII, and hastily replaced on the decor of the Royal palaces at Greenwich, Nonesuch and Hampton Court by the arms of her successor, Jane Seymour, after Anne's execution. Henry VIII built elaborate new mews for his hawks, and they were extended even more elaborately after they had been gutted by fire in 1593. Historian John Stow considered this structure so essentially one of the sights of London that he carefully chronicled both its loss and its renovation. Queen Elizabeth I carried on the family passion for hawking. By her day the term hawker had become associated with any form of itinerant pedlar, though originally it was coined to apply only to those travelling salesmen specialising in the sale of sporting birds. The hawker's associate, the hunt servant, who carried the frame on which the hooded birds perched until required, was technically known as a cadger. This was one of the most menial tasks, and, through the ages, the word has come to mean all who beg or scrounge a living from others.

The death knell of falconry was sounded by the introduction of the sporting gun towards the end of the seventeenth century, though in remoter parts of the world, such as the Middle East and northern India, hunting with hawks persisted as a regular sport for the relatively well-to-do almost into the space age. In the 1970s there seems to be a minority revival of interest in falconry, partly inspired by the desire to ensure that predatory species are not wiped out. A falconry centre has been established at Newent, near Gloucester, where training in falconry and demonstrations for visitors are provided; and under the auspices of the Council for Small Industries in Rural Areas, the Newmarket leather goods firm of Boyce & Rogers is currently busy turning out falconers' gloves and hawks' hoods that are almost as popular as curios for tourists as they are for use by the growing number of falconers. The great dovekeeping cult also has roots in the Dark Ages. Plans for the Abbey of St Gall in France, drawn up in the ninth century, show a round hen pen and round duck pen in the monks' garden, and a house between them for the keeper of this valuable communal property.

Modern falconer's glove

The abbeys, with their tradition of hospitality to all travellers and responsibility not only for the care of the sick, aged and poor of their parish, but their own community as well, needed to be efficient farmers. Their settled way of life, of course, allowed them not only to develop skills in horticulture, agriculture and stock-keeping, but—perhaps even more important— to maintain an oral tradition of scholarship. They also built up libraries for the benefit of the next generation of novices and to disseminate practical and spiritual knowledge among houses of the same order.

It is likely that long before the Norman Conquest of England the monks had already discovered the usefulness of a pigeon loft as a means of ensuring year-round meat supplies in an economy where it was the usual practice to kill off all but the breeding stock each autumn. In spring, of course, a pigeon loft would supplement monastic menus with the delicacy of pigeon eggs and squabs taken directly from the nest before flight. However, all direct evidence of monastic pigeon-loft building is post-Conquest, when the Normans had replaced wood by stone in ecclesiastical building.

The Dove House at Haddenham, Buckinghamshire, built in 1100, is reputed to be one of the oldest dovecotes, though a 540-hole roost dovecote in the priory garden just outside Dunster, Somerset, runs it a close second. Although the roof was replaced in the eighteenth century, the Dunster dovecote has a fine interior, preserved in much the same condition as its heyday, with the portenance or potence, the revolving ladder used by the dove keeper to tend his stock, still in good working order.

Another impressive dovecote, whose cross-shaped glassless windows suggest a monastic origin, can be seen in southern England at Bemerton, a few miles west of Salisbury, Wiltshire. This is in the classic form of a round tower with holes near the eaves for the entry of the birds and a door at the base for the birdkeeper. Entry to early dovecotes is usually via a flight of steps as a precaution against animal raiders, principally foxes.

This style of building usually has a central vent in the roof for ventilation, and also to provide light for the dove keeper, while its conical shape ensures that the occupants do not get wet. The basic shape of permanent

dovecotes changed very little over the 800 odd years during which they were regularly in use, so it is difficult to date them except by relating them to surrounding buildings, or by discovering documentary evidence.

At the time of the English Reformation with its distribution of monastic estates, the acquisition of pigeon lofts or dovecotes, recognised as real profit-makers for their owners, was hotly disputed by the local gentry. Many a dovecote that had formerly been part of a farmyard complex then became a garden or parkland feature of the squire's mansion. One example was the great dove house at Athelhampton, Dorset. It is a 1,000-bird dovecote, one of the largest still viewable for the public in Britain, and is currently in process of restoration, which will include repair of the portenance, the lead roof and the antique weather vane.

A typical Tudor structure, with nest boxes for 1,500 pigeons, was that erected by Sir John Gostwick, Cardinal Wolsey's Master of Horse, at Willington, 4 miles east of Bedford. Building a dovecote during this period was a restricted right, and one which, moreover, considerably annoyed those yeoman farmers on whose lands m'lord's pigeons feasted before returning to his loft to roost.

Almost certainly Catherine de Medici, who on her marriage to Henri II of France, carried so many of her Florentine customs to her adopted country, was responsible for the spate of dovecote construction in France in the sixteenth century. There is, for example, an elaborate decorative dovecote in the grounds of the Château Talcy, which was built in 1520 for her cousin Bernard de Saviate. More practical French pigeon lofts can be seen at the Château de Foullertorte (St George sur Erve) and René Thory's Château de Boumouis (St Martin de la Place, Maine et Loire). The former château belongs to the age of the fortified house, despite the late date of its construction—1570. It is a grim-looking granite pile, completely surrounded by moats fed from the River Erve. In this sort of setting the provision of a home for livestock which could safely sally forth to feed each day and return literally over the heads of besiegers

Stone dovecote at Bemerton, Wiltshire

Dove house at Athelhampton, Dorset

22

was an obvious advantage. The latter château has one of the largest and most complete of early French dovecotes, still to be seen today, and contemporary with the house, which was completed in 1515. The dovecote is approached by a winding staircase and has 1,200 pigeonholes.

Dovecote building became something of a mania with English landowners from 1500 until the Civil War. 'No kingdom of the worlde hath so many dove houses,' wrote Fynes Moryson, a Jacobean traveller; and Samuel Hartlib, author of *The Discourse on Husbandry* (1651), wrote to his friend, the poet Milton, 'pigeons are now a hurtful fowle by reason of their multitude and the number of houses erected daille for their increase'. He estimated that there were 26,000 English dovecotes.

'Allowing 500 birds to each house and assuming each pair consume four bushels of grain yearly, the annual waste amounts to an incredible sum', he complained. Certainly the ethics of pigeon keepers left much to be desired. In addition to expecting their neighbours to supply the fodder, loft owners were not above trying to lure further pairs from nearby pigeon owners. A favourite, and strictly illegal, trick was to whitewash the exterior of the loft to make it more clearly visible. Much less salubrious were some of the recipes for infallible pigeon lures that circulated among the country gentry, such as the use of a 'baked and salted cat', or 'pigeon pudding' heavily laced with cummin seed.

The accession of James VI of Scotland to the English throne in 1603 probably helped to spread dovekeeping into Scotland, where there are some of the finest old dovecotes still in existence: one such is at Polmont, 2 miles east of Falkirk, which was erected in 1647 and bears the arms of its original owner, William Livingstone, over the door.

The seventeenth century saw the expansion of the dovecote craze into the more remote corners of the British Isles; new methods of building dovecotes were adopted, an early example being the use of a square tower with domed vault and hexagonal cupola in the Penmon dovecote near Beaumaris, Anglesey (Wales), which was completed in 1600.

Toward the middle of the seventeenth century English yeomen farmers began to take up dovekeeping, often incorporating pigeon shelters in the

Seventeenth-century dovecote at Grassington, Yorkshire

framework of the farmhouse itself—as at the seventeenth-century farm-house just outside Grassington, Yorkshire.

Meanwhile up at the manor dovecotes were changing from small factory farms into garden conceits. This process was complete by the time the gardens of the Château de Villesavin, Tour en Sologne, Loire et Cher, were designed. Here the seventeenth-century dovecote is designed to harmonise with the white marble fountains that are the major feature of the grounds. The ultimate switch of the dovecote from use to ornament occurs in the gardens of the Château de Canon, which were remodelled in the eighteenth century for a close friend of Voltaire. These gardens are famous for their chartreuses—squares surrounded by thick green-clad walls and filled with flowers in springtime—and are positively littered with toy dovecotes as well as busts, statues and miniature temples, both classical and Chinese in style.

Almost 200 years later, in the 1920s, trendy garden planners rediscovered the dovecote, and Gertrude Jekyll included half a dozen plans for structures to take up to three pairs of birds in her lavishly illustrated *Garden Ornament*, published in 1928. This rediscovery happily reminded owners of antique dovecotes of their worth, and Nymans, Sussex, is a marvellous example of the use of a Tudor dovecote as the centrepiece of early twentieth-century landscape gardening. At Rousham and Chastleton House, Oxfordshire; Bingham's Melcombe, Dorset; Eardisland and Old Sufton, Herefordshire; Wynyates, Warwickshire; Quenington Nauton and Daglingworth, Gloucestershire; Charleston Manor, Sussex; and Fyfield in Wilts there are also impressive dovecotes from Tudor times, if not earlier.

An interesting comment on the number of pigeons accommodated today compared with the past was shown by the National Trust in 1962. That body decided to restore and restock the dovecote at Cotehele House, Cornwall, and considered two pairs of fantails sufficient for a building originally designed for 2,000 birds.

In addition to their excursions into pigeon breeding, the monks of the Middle Ages raised swans for the table. Chaucer, whose observant eye noted an early British passion for bird-eating as well as birdkeeping, makes the monk taking the famous pilgrimage to Canterbury lick his lips at the mere mention of roast swan. The most spectacular of surviving monastic swanneries in Britain is on the Chesil Bank, at Abbotsbury, Dorset. It was first mentioned in the court rolls of the manor of Abbotsbury, which became, as the name suggests, a monastic institution in 1393. In choosing Abbotsbury the aviculturist was using natural resources to his own advantage. The abundance of the *zostera marina* and *zostera nana* seaweeds in the Fleet and the narrow lagoon-like strip of water lying between the shingles of the Chesil Bank and the mainland make the site a feeding ground for flocks of wild mute swans, which over the years have attained some degree of domestication. The exact number present at Abbotsbury is dependent on how kind weather conditions are to the development of these marine plants. In severe winters, when the Fleet freezes over, the swan is separated from his food by the ice; and after the thaw food is also in very short supply for a while, since the weed has been trapped in the ice and pulled up by the roots on the rising tide.

Thus the number of swans at Abbotsbury can vary from as few as 300 to as many as 1,500. The 1971 survey, however, of around 500 birds is approximately the same number as was logged in 1541, when the swannery passed at the Reformation from the Church to the new lord of the manor, Sir Giles Strangeways.

Although they are called 'mute', the swans at Abbotsbury, and those in most of the other swanneries of the British Isles, can in fact communicate with each other by a series of hisses and snorts. They mate for life and, barring accident, live for around forty years. The mute swan lays two to nine eggs in May. The cygnets hatch in five to six weeks and enter the water at two days old. They stay within the family group for a further seven months, by which time they weigh 20 lb and can fly. Their feathers, however, remain grey-brown until they are a year old, at which stage they leave their parents. They do not become mature enough to mate until they are four years old.

Since the eighteenth century the deeds of the Abbotsbury swannery have been held by the Earls of Ilchester, who appoint the curator, known still as the 'swanherd'. This title has been in the family of the present holder, Fred Lexster, for three generations.

Although most swans in Britain are considered crown property, those on the Thames are equally divided between the Vintners Company, the Dyers Company and the monarch, and the need to classify cygnets has given rise to a colourful ceremony known as 'swan upping', which takes place in the third week of July: the Swan Wardens of the two livery companies then cut nicks in the beaks of the swans so that they can be recognised in future. The Dyers' swans have one nick, the Vintners' two, while the sovereign's are unmarked. Over the years, numerous pubs named Swan with Two Nicks, indicating that they were the property of a vintner (an obvious advantage for licensed premises), have had their names corrupted into 'Swan with Two Necks' by a public no doubt puzzled at the original name.

Roast swan is the traditional dish of honour at livery company banquets, which follow the swan-upping ceremony. It is still also served at ritual feasts in a number of Oxford colleges. Today the swans for roasting will almost certainly have come from Messrs Pettits of Reedham, who are one of the few poultry firms still dealing with swan meat; their supplier is the City of Norwich, which retains its ancient right to operate a swan pit for profit. First mention of the Norwich swan pit comes in a document of 1487 which lists a payment to one William Bylney, 'pro custodia cignorum' at St Giles Hospital. In the 1970s swan herding is a secondary duty of the Norwich city engineer's department, whose swan population is held at twenty-five pairs, each of which is encouraged to rear a full clutch of eight nestlings a year.

Most of the young swans not required to keep up the Norwich numbers are sent to parks and wild-life reserves, or presented to private owners who can prove that they have a suitable lake or other watery accommodation in their grounds. The idea of giving swans away would have certainly shocked the founders of the Norwich pits in the Middle Ages, for during the reign of Edward III swan-keeping was a privilege reserved for those who already possessed a freehold to the value of 5 marks, a considerable sum for those days, and one which reserved this form of aviculture for the rich.

In the year 1272 such extortionate prices were being charged for table swans in the City of London that the corporation fixed their price at 3s. For a comparative poulterer's price-scale, compare the fact that a goose was then priced at 2½d. Whatever their price, however, it is unlikely that there will ever be a revival of interest in swan as a table bird. For the modern palate, used to blander flavours, the strong smelling, darkly fishy flesh of swan, which needs a great deal of mastication to make it tender, is the antithesis of a treat.

ⁿⁿⁿⁿⁿⁿⁿⁿⁿⁿⁿⁿⁿⁿⁿⁿⁿⁿⁿⁿⁿⁿⁿⁿⁿⁿⁿⁿⁿⁿⁿⁿⁿ

CHAPTER TWO
Renaissance Exoticism and After

ⁿⁿⁿⁿⁿⁿⁿⁿⁿⁿⁿⁿⁿⁿⁿⁿⁿⁿⁿⁿⁿⁿⁿⁿⁿⁿⁿⁿⁿⁿⁿⁿⁿ

The explosive quality of the Renaissance created an ideal climate for the spread of aviculture. The rediscovery of the classical world, with its love of villa gardening, helped make exotic birdkeeping once again a cult for the rich and famous. Another boost for aviculture was the appreciation, with the departure of the Moors from Spain, of the culture they left behind them; and along with the architecture and algebra, the Moorish legacy included a passion for walled gardens in which aviaries of singing birds were as popular as the flowers and fountains themselves. Contemporary records speak with wonder of the rare-bird aviary established by Abd-er Rahman III at his palace near Cordova. His example was no doubt copied all over Spanish colonies by gentlemen of wealth and influence.

The domes that embellished their homes and mosques were reproduced in miniature in Moorish birdcages, creating a pattern which persists to this day in North Africa in the delicate ball-topped cage beloved as a souvenir of Tunisia by all visitors to that country. Local skill in wire-working, combined with traditionally abstract patterns such as the arabesque, which were the principal art motifs of a people whose religion forbade the reproduction of the living form, helped to make these cages objects of beauty as well as utility.

28

Likewise the skill in ceramic work developed in the typically Moorish tilings was pressed into service in the construction of bird homes. This tradition was to linger in Spain even after the Moors had been expelled, and was in turn carried by Spanish conquerors into the Low Countries, creating a Dutch tradition of cage manufacture that continues into the present century.

Even more important than either of these facets of the changing world of the Renaissance, however, was the opening up of new trade routes, with better opportunities than ever for collecting and bringing back live birds. It was the Portugese trading fleets that first brought the canary to Europe to found its dynasty of domesticated cage birds—ultimately very different in colour, conformation and habit from their wild finch forebears.

Meanwhile the discovery of the 'New World' added to the list of exotic birds that rich aviary owners wished to acquire. A pair of Cuban Amazon parrots, for instance, were carried in Columbus's triumphant welcome-

Peacocks in the Renaissance garden from Fior de Vertu, *Venice, 1531*

29

home procession through the streets of Barcelona, and from there found their way into the royal bird collection of his patron, Queen Isabella of Spain.

The changing pattern of court existence, initiated in Italy in the four-teenth century and fanning outwards through the whole of Europe over the next 200 years, made possible the foundation of vast menageries, such as the collection at Schönbrunn, Austria, founded in 1552 by the Emperor Maximilian II, which were later to be the basis of great public zoos.

As long as warfare and local feuds remained endemic, and were a matter of the bow and arrow or siege engine, the homes of the rich remained draughty fortified castles, with no scope for garden aviary construction, and, within the house, the worst possible conditions for the maintenance of chamber birds. When the countryside became more settled, and the invention of cannon rendered the castles pregnable, however, there was no longer any reason for the rich to suffer such discomfort, and much of the cash previously spent on their self-preservation was diverted to the beautification of their surroundings. Moreover the rising merchant classes sought to impress their neighbours by the magnificence of their style of living, and in so doing patronised not only the artist, goldsmith, architect and furniture designer, but the suppliers of all forms of luxury. In an age of renewed curiosity about the wonders of the world beyond one's own little kingdom, the maintenance of a menagerie of rare animals and birds was considered almost a duty for the ruling class. 'It belongs to the position of the great,' wrote Matarazzo, 'to keep horses, dogs, mules, falcons, exotic birds, court jesters and singers.'

This was a precept on which Lorenzo de Medici, for one, was eager to act. The designs commissioned from Giulio di San Gallo for the Poggio a Cajano palace, some 10 miles outside Florence, started in 1485, make it clear through marginal notes in the future owner's own hand that the layout of the grounds must include provision for Lorenzo's private zoo and rare-bird collection.

A century later when the Villa d'Este, at Tivoli just outside Rome, was being prepared for Cardinal Ferrara by Pirro Ligorio, no aviary was included in the plans; but the need for bird noises to complete the sophisticated pleasure of the garden was acknowledged in the decision to include, among the many exotic 'waterworks' of the gardens, a fountain/ water organ whose playing simulated the songs of small birds. Later still, in 1618, when the gardens of the Villa Borghese were being planned by Rainaldi for Scipione Borghese, a nephew of Pope Paul V, an aviary was once again a vital part of the scheme.

Even as early as the late thirteenth century aviary construction was included in all the best Italian gardening books. For example, Pietro Crescenzi's *Opus Ruralium Commodurum*, which first appeared in manuscript form at this time, then went into print in a Latin edition, and was translated into French, German and Italian in 1471, carries the following instructions: 'At the top of some small trees let there be built a kind of house having a roof and walls of copper wire, finely netted, where shall be put pheasants, partridges, nightingales, blackbirds, goldfinches, linnets and all kinds of singing birds.' Crescenzi adds, very sensibly, that it is best to site the aviary in such a position that it can be enjoyed from the windows of the house as well as from the gardens.

His selection of birds concentrates on native European types easily obtainable by trapping, but in his Vivarium the Emperor Frederick II is reported to have kept both cranes and pelicans, though he was 'most proud' of a white cockatoo presented to him by 'The Sultan of Babylon'.

In the splendid ducal palace built in the 1460s by Luciano Laurana for Federico da Montefeltro at Urbino (northern Italy) bird motifs dominate the decor. Not only is the eagle seen everywhere as the heraldic sign of the Montefeltro family, but in the Duke's own 'studiolo', his private apartment, is a famous trompe d'oeil cupboard showing a pair of caged parrots. Their cage can be seen in a corner of the room in contrasted light and dark wood marquetry; it is hexagonal and horizontally barred, with conical roof and suspension hook, and each corner of the eaves is topped by a ball-shaped decoration.

Parrots fascinated their Renaissance owners, both for their brilliant colours and for their ability to mimic the human voice. In Elizabethan

Painting of German bird fancier—'Der Vogelfreund'

times the word 'popinjay', the colloquialism for a parrot, began to be applied to those young men of fashion whose fancy for gay clothing bordered on the vulgar or the effeminate.

Despite her constant progresses round her kingdom, the garden-conscious Virgin Queen probably maintained aviaries at most of her principal residences. Pheasants were probably the usual inmates, these being hand-reared in the aviaries of Henry VIII's Eltham Palace. Household accounts of the period show that their French keeper received a payment of 9s 4d for his trouble from the King's Privy Purse.

That aviaries were relatively commonplace in well-to-do gardens can be gleaned from Bacon's essay *On Gardens*, written in 1597: 'For aviaries I like them not, except they be of that largeness as they may be turfed and have living plants and bushes set in them: that the birds may have more scope and natural nesting, and that no foulness appear on the floor of the aviary'.

A popular species in Tudor times, since it was both eatable and decorative, was the peacock. A liberty peacock strutting about the lawns of his country estate was something of a status symbol for the Tudor landowner. Also Andrew Boorde's cookbook, published in 1562, has several recipes for roasting peacock. These birds featured regularly in the price listings of markets like London's Leadenhall. For the year 1413 London vendors quote them for the pot at 1s per bird, but the price must have risen by Tudor times.

Really rich Tudor bird fanciers may well have owned canaries, for the island of Madeira had been a Portuguese possession since 1420, and the birds were exported. By the time Gesner wrote his *Historia Animalium* in 1555, the canary was a sufficiently familiar captive for him to include notes on its diet: 'line seed and poppy seed and sometimes millet. They delight in sugar and sugar cane, and also in that sort of chickweed or mousear which is commonly called henbit'. This advice would be regarded as sound even in the 1970s. Gesner likens the canary to the 'citril': 'similar to this is, as I hear, the bird of sweetest song, called canary which is brought from the Canary Islands'.

c   33

The first of the canary exports were birds of the olive-green plumage still to be found among the Canary Islands wildlings. It was not until the seventeenth century that the clear yellow shade we talk of today as 'canary yellow' became a feature of the breed. Legend has it that a shipment of finches escaped as a result of a shipwreck on the Isle of Elba during a journey which should have ended at the port of Leghorn. All the birds in the shipment were cocks, since they were to be sold as songsters. After their release, they found themselves local mates, and, on recapture, together with their newly raised families, they were found to have produced yellow offspring.

Anyone with a knowledge of canary breeding, however, is tempted to regard this pretty story as mere myth, since the bulk of canary-finch crossbreeds—and admittedly canaries will mate and rear young with most members of the finch family—are sterile. Such hybrids are still regularly bred by fanciers, for in both plumage and song they can pick up the virtues of both parents and make excellent exhibition specimens. Their inability to reproduce themselves traditionally labels them as mules.

In only one instance—the twentieth-century crossing of the canary and the South American siskin—has the union been fruitful enough to create a whole new strain. This is the subspecies called red factor—now established as a canary type—whose plumage can be pink, orange, apricot or tomato-tinted, and who now breed these colours of canary freely without need for backcrossing to their siskin heritage. It seems more likely, therefore, that the change to yellow was the result of careful selective breeding from those canary–finch individuals whose plumage was more yellow than most.

From the first the pure yellow canary was in demand as a parlour pet among fanciers, though the achievement of particular markings, such as those of colour-capped spangled birds, still available today and known as lizards, was always more interesting than simply getting a clear coloured specimen. Quite early in the history of canary keeping the fancy itself

Typical cages for roller canaries

split into those breeders, such as the pioneers of the Norwich strain, whose primary aim was a show bird of handsome proportions and feathering, and those, like the Harz mountains fanciers, who concentrated from the first on perfection of voice.

Harz mountain rollers have predominantly green plumage to this day, and are called rollers from their ability to hold and roll a single note of their song. American fanciers, differentiating between rollers and the rest, describe them as either warblers or choppers.

Although singing is natural to all canaries, the voice of the prize roller is as different from the ordinary canary's as an opera singer's from the bathroom warbler. Roller song is taught: when young birds are first

German cage, dated 1757

A GERMAN CAGE WITH THE CREST OF FRANKFURT (MAIN).
IT IS DATED 1757.

ON LOAN FROM MRS. E.E. PHILIPP, LONDON.

coming into song, they are placed in darkened boxes round the cage of an expert adult singer, whom they learn to copy. Today attempts are being made to train young rollers with tape recorders; in the seventeenth century some of the earliest musical-box automata were 'bird-organ' hurdy-gurdies which were used to stimulate the song of prize canaries during training. Nightingales might also be employed as roller tutors, as indeed were various ingenious machines. The song of a prize roller can be divided into thirteen distinct song passages, known in show circles as rolls and tours. There are five rolls—bass roll, hollow roll, glucke roll, water roll, bell roll—and eight tours—water glucke tour, glucke tour, koller tour, flutes tour, schockel tour, hollow bell tour, deep bubbling water tour and bell tour.

The centre of the Harz mountains canary-breeding region is the little town of St Andreasburgh. Before the arrival of the canary cult, the craftsmen of the district were famous for the quality of their wood carving, and they applied their traditional techniques to the housing of the birds that were to make their region famous. Their cages, now prized as antiques, look like mountain chalets in miniature, taking forms strongly reminiscent of elaborate and expensive cuckoo-clock cases. This similarity is heightened by the fact that in order to control the bird's song, especially during contests or exhibitions, the breeder uses the natural habit of the bird to roost during darkness and wake to a dawn chorus. The exhibition cage is therefore equipped with tiny wooden doors that can blot out the daylight until the bird is required to sing—which it will do, on cue, when the doors are opened.

The expertise in the breeding and management of song canaries was acknowledged by fanciers all over Europe as early as 1655 when J. B. Gent wrote of the 'plentiful breeding of canaries in Germany and Italy'. In his *Epitome of Husbandry*, published in 1675, Joseph Blagrove comments: 'Now with industry they breed them (canaries) very plentifully, and the German birds in handsomeness and song excell those brought from the Canaries'.

One reason for the success of the roller canary was the way it was

Wire birdcage of the 1670s

packed for export. Rather in the same way as the functional straw wrap of the Chianti bottle, itself another example of supremely practical protection, became an easily recognisable piece of point-of-sale advertising, so the traditional double-doored cage of the Harz mountains canary not only enabled it to travel safely and arrive in good condition, but represented an attractive means of recognising the genuine product.

It was the Low Countries' fanciers who concentrated on the production of the 'show' canary, which was brought to Britain by Protestant refugees. The canary-breeding centres of East Anglia, especially the Norwich region, show where these refugees settled.

Canaries kept by seventeenth-century Dutch burghers were, like the plate, rugs and other rich household effects, a symbol of trading wealth. The birds were splendidly housed in cages that made free use of such precious materials as ebony or ivory and contained handsome blown glass or fancy ceramic feeding pots. Variations on a bell-shaped theme were most favoured by Dutch cage designers, though sometimes this basic form was broken up into a series of tiers which could, in the finest examples, be given the classical trimmings of balustrades and columns in miniature. Hanging cages were often further embellished with silken tassels or lustres hanging from their base.

Paintings of the period reveal that seventeenth-century Dutch houses were far cleaner than French or British, and the frequent cleaning and scrubbing which Dutch birdcages were subjected to made ceramic surfaces popular. Dutch cleanliness undoubtedly helped in the successful breeding and rearing of birds whose appeal depended on their fine appearance.

The fervour for birdkeeping gripped all classes, and on a visit to Holland in 1634 Sir William Brereton specially noted the Prince of Orange's famous garden aviary. 'The fairest and most spacious plot I ever saw' included an aviary stocked with 'all manner of dainty fowl', wrote Sir William.

Perhaps it was his years in exile on the Continent that helped to turn the Stuart king, Charles II of England, into a bird fancier. His grandfather, James I, had established a wildfowl collection in St James Park, London,

that initially included ospreys, gannets and cormorants. It was left to Charles II to so line the adjoining street with the cages containing his feathered friends that ever since the thoroughfare has been known as Birdcage Walk. The spectacle of the Merry Monarch, a bevy of his favourite spaniels at his heels, and quite possibly a famous beauty on his arm, strolling along the walk during the afternoon to feed its inhabitants was one of the sights of Restoration London. The main attraction for the members of the public, and apparently the favourite bird of the king himself, was a crane which, having suffered an accident in its youth, had been fitted with a wooden leg.

Royal interest in, and patronage of, birdkeeping encouraged the nobility to build garden aviaries, and Ham House, near Richmond, Surrey, built in 1610, was said by the diarist John Evelyn to be equipped with a large aviary.

The other famous English diarist of the seventeenth century, Samuel Pepys, was also eager to record the fashion for birdkeeping. He writes excitedly of the pair of canaries presented to him by his friend Captain Rooth of Dartmouth, 'a seafaring man', and on 25 January 1661 notes, 'two cages bought this evening for my canary birds have been delivered'. On 11 January 1665 he sadly records the death of his treasured pets, but his interest in birdkeeping remained constant, for some eighteen months later, when visiting the garden of Lord Brooke in Hackney, London, he remarks, somewhat acidly: 'The house was not good, nor the prospect, but the gardens were excellent. I saw a great variety of exotic plants, several labyrinths and a pretty aviary'.

Presumably, as a man of fashion Pepys housed his canaries in a handsome Dutch-style cage. Many Stuart bird lovers, however, were content to use simple rush structures, such as the lantern-like specimen carved on the tomb of the seventeenth-century poet Sir John Suckling in St Andrew's Church, Norwich. The choice of a bird winging its way from a cage as a symbol of the soul's release from death has special interest, since in a

Dutch bell-shaped cage, 1600–1650, now in Utrecht museum

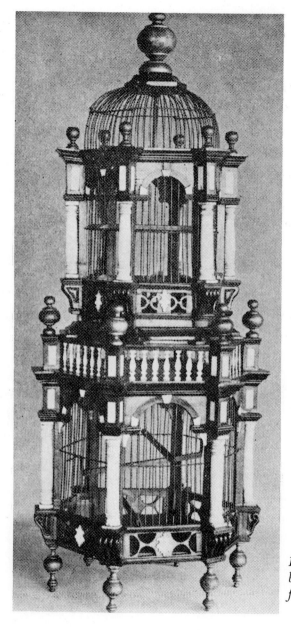

Elaborate 'classical' birdcage of the type favoured by early Dutch fanciers

canary-conscious town like Norwich it almost certainly reproduced a cage and pet bird well known to the mason.

When the British throne passed to Charles' niece Mary and her Dutch husband William, the vogue for keeping pet birds was once again stimulated by royal interest. During her sojourn in Holland one of Mary's favourite retreats had been the Château Sorgvliet on the road to Schevering, a property belonging to the Duke of Portland and famous for its aviary of cranes. There was, moreover, an extensive menagerie and aviary in the grounds of Honslaerdyck, situated between the Hague and the Hook of Holland, and reputed to be the finest seat in the Netherlands. It was without question the favourite palace of William III.

CHAPTER THREE

The Age of Elegance

Birdkeeping on a grand scale, as an attraction in the grounds of a 'stately home', developed with the changing fashions in landscape gardening in the eighteenth century. During the late seventeenth and very early eighteenth centuries garden planning was largely influenced by the French: families of fashion aimed at transforming their ancestral seats into miniature Versailles, organising their grounds as formal combinations of parterres, arcades and watercourses, which allowed little scope for the introduction of aviaries. But from the middle of the eighteenth century, when the English concept of the garden as a park came into fashion, the garden aviary assumed more importance than ever before.

The English style revolved round the apparent informality of trees and lawns sweeping up to the doors of the mansion itself. This carefully contrived natural look needed animals to complete the picture. So herds of deer (English native and exotic), sheep and cattle were introduced into these garden pastures, performing coincidentally the useful task of keeping the grass clipped in the days before the lawn-mower. The beasts were restrained from advancing to the doors of the house itself by the sunken ditch known as the ha-ha, which was now developed.

The need for animal life was also felt by European noblemen when they abandoned the canals, square ponds and deity-filled fountains previously beloved by the master gardeners of France and Italy in favour of 'natural' artificial lakes, such as the Serpentine in London's Hyde Park, and the lake in the classically eighteenth-century scenic gardens of Stourhead, Wiltshire. They wanted their informal waters adorned with appropriate wildfowl, and if the waterfowl could not be persuaded to stay by the almost ideal 'natural' conditions the informal lake provided, then they were confined in aviaries, whose architecture was tailormade to provide picturesque vistas from the windows of the great house.

It is typical of the eighteenth century that when the grounds of Peter the Great's Mon Plaisir palace at Peterhof in Russia were being changed, by Quarenghi in 1789, from their formal Dutch style to the English look, an aviary should have been included among the amenities. Another Russian ruler, Catherine the Great, was not only interested in singing-bird automata (see page 53), but was a keen ornithologist who added aviaries to most of her major palace grounds.

Interest in the larger birds, and especially fancy pheasants from China, was stimulated by the general fashion for 'Chinoiserie' later in the century. The Gothic style followed the Chinese influence, though there remained a strong Palladian classical school in architecture and landscaping, and in consequence aviaries may come in any of these styles—or sometimes in a wild mixture of all three. For example, the aviary at Knole, near Sevenoaks, Kent, the home of the Sackvilles since Tudor times, though designed to house Chinese pheasants was built in the Gothic style; it is set in a little hollow, which also houses a sham Gothic ruin, hard by the former kitchen garden of the great house. The aviary itself is octagonal, as is the conical roof that seems almost to have been inspired by the local oasthouses. The building has twin towers and a chapel-like entry. Over the double doors decorated with lion masks is a niche containing the wooden statuette of a red-robed monk.

Eighteenth-century pheasants were housed much better than eighteenth-century peasants. At Knole, in fact, for the past 100 years the aviary has served to house one of the park rangers and his family. Only the name-

Kew aviary, eighteenth century

plate 'The Birdhouse' on the garden gate serves as a reminder of the purpose for which it was constructed in 1761. It might seem likely that its chimney pots were added to make life more comfortable for its human occupants, but not so. Records show that Knole was one of the first artificially heated aviaries, its warmth enabling no fewer than twenty-three species of exotic birds to be successfully maintained.

The builder of The Birdhouse was almost certainly that same Lord Amherst whose interest in ornithology is perpetuated by the scientific name *Phasianus Amherstiae*, for the species of decorative pheasant which he was the first to introduce from China, where he served for a number of years as British Ambassador. A small interior court at Knole is called the Pheasant Court, because Lord Amherst maintained his gamebirds there.

One might have expected the Chinese style to prevail in the design of the aviary at Kew, since a mock Chinese pagoda dominates the landscape. Princess Augusta commissioned this aviary, for the grounds of Kew Palace, near London (now the Royal Botanical Gardens), from William Chambers, but it has long since disappeared. Indeed it had disappeared by the 1840s when conservatory building, for which Kew is more famous, proliferated. Contemporary prints of the structure are still extant and reveal it to have been single-storied in the classical style, not Chinese, with an octagonal domed centre section. It was used to house exotic waterfowl.

Not surprisingly in an age when aviaries were royally patronised and ultra-fashionable there was considerable rivalry both in Britain and on the European continent over bird collections. It is possible to study many of the most famous aviaries of the eighteenth century only through prints and engravings—so often made as souvenirs of the 'grand tour'; the majority of the actual buildings have fallen victim to passing time or changing tastes in garden architecture.

Prints tell us what we know of the aviary on the Morfontaine estate near Chantilly, where the famous revolutionary treaty of friendship between France and America was first signed; the garden was laid out on waste land in the 1770s, the aviary being a semicircular colonnaded structure. Probably because its neo-classic style was to remain in favour for the first two decades of the nineteenth century, the aviary was still surviving when Morfontaine became the favourite residence of Joseph Bonaparte. He mentions in his letters the regret he felt at abandoning the pleasures of his garden—including, one must suppose, its bird collection—when he accepted the crown of Naples in 1806.

Prints also tell us something of the occupants as well as the form of the famous Westerhof aviary in Holland. The landscaped garden with an aviary as its central feature dates from the early eighteenth century. The aviary itself consisted of a sunken courtyard with, at its heart, an octagonal house for small birds. The court itself was intended to provide an exercise area for large birds, most of which seem to have been cranes of various types. The central bird house is topped by a bronze figure of an eagle about to take flight. This bird of prey appeared on the top of octagonal and bell-shaped cages for small singing birds well into the nineteenth century. The figure of an eagle can still be seen topping the birds-of-prey

Dutch aviary with cranes, early eighteenth century

range of housing at the London Zoo where, incongruously, a London pigeon or sparrow is usually to be found using it as a perch.

One of the most spectacular layouts, vulgar even to contemporary observers, was the garden and aviary range built for James Brydges, Duke of Chandos, at Cánons in Middlesex in the early eighteenth century. The garden boasted three avenues 1,303 yd, 1,000 yd and 808 yd long, and water for the numerous fountains and plants was piped from Stanmore, a distance of nearly 3 miles.

Accommodation and the variety of birds to be viewed in the gardens was on the same plane of magnificence. A Mr J. Macky who visited the gardens in 1722 noted that the owner had imported 'barrow ducks, storks, wild geese from Barbados, whistling ducks and flamingos from Antigua'. There were also ostriches, blue macaws, virginia fowls, song birds and 'eagles which drank out of specially carved stone basins'.

The Duke of Devonshire's collection at Chiswick contained giraffes, elephants, kangaroos and several emus.

Rich bird collectors in the eighteenth century were also keen ornithologists—despite the oft-quoted opinion then that 'the proper study for mankind is man'—and eager readers of books on birds. In fact, patrons would encourage their birdkeepers to set down in print their findings as a guide for future generations of aviculturists; and some of these authors were both popular and expert. For example, J. M. Bechstein's *Cage and Chamber Birds*, which first appeared in 1794, continued as a bestseller among 'the fancy' in various editions up to the start of World War I.

In 1709 the first standard work on the canary, Hervieux's *Traité des Serin de Canarie*, was published; the author was then employed as 'inspector of canary breeding' by the Duchess of Berry. He lists twenty-nine distinctively coloured and marked strains, all developed from original wild Canary Islands green finches.

Apart from birdkeeping, eighteenth-century garden planners built birdcage-like follies—for human dalliance. The most famous surviving example is at Melbourne Hall, Derbyshire—the 'Birdcage', constructed between 1708 and 1711 by blacksmith Robert Bakewell. Its elaborate

Pair of porcelain canaries on appleblossom, made at Worcester in the eighteenth century

wrought ironwork happily marries scroll, bar and naturalistic repoussé work in leaf and fruit motifs.

Another manifestation of eighteenth-century interest in birds was the proliferation of bird ornaments for chimneypiece and china cabinet: one example, the charming pair of yellow canaries perched on a spray of appleblossom, one of the Worcester factory's bestselling lines in the 1770s, can be seen in the Dyson Perrins Museum, Severn Street, Worcester. Birds had been popular motifs on domestic as well as decorative ware from the inception of the Worcester plant in the 1750s; pheasant and mallard decorations were among the favourite motifs, though one popular service featured a macaw in natural colours on the cups and saucers. Worcester, incidentally, still include bird statues among their range for collectors, and to meet the taste of the 1970s the canary has now been joined by 6 in figures of blue and green budgerigars.

Mostly, however, its eighteenth-century birds were presented in the Chinese manner, since most of the porcelain of the period directly imitated imported oriental wares, and there was a general vogue for the Chinese style. Many bird motifs also appeared on household textiles and wallpapers, the dove being specially popular. Designers in these fields probably often referred to the colour plates of Eleazar Albin, whose album *Turtle Doves from the East Indies* first appeared in 1735.

As well as bird motifs, many eighteenth-century items of ornamental porcelain showing rustic figures of shepherds and shepherdesses included pet birds and birdcages. Enoch Wood, who was active at Burslem during the 1750s, specialised in this line, though it was also a favourite with the Bow factories. Figures holding birdcages remained popular until the rise of the cheap Staffordshire statuette—a particularly fine example of a Pratt-ware figure of this type was auctioned as part of the break-up of the famous Pugh collection in London in 1971. Such figures give a clear idea of the kind of cages in which ordinary citizens kept their pets and show that the square-sided lantern cage, which had first made its appearance in the seventeenth century, was still in use as late as 1800.

Meanwhile birdcages for the rich were being made in a wide range of

(left) *Enoch Wood statuette, eighteenth century;* (right) *Pratt-ware statuette of girl with birdcage, English, early nineteenth century*

materials. In the elegant drawing room, seed-scattering was a problem, and to solve this the Duchess of Devonshire commissioned, in 1771, a patent cage made of glass. The floor and roof were of moulded cut Waterford crystal inset in a burnished steel rim, which was joined top and bottom by steel angles that held the polished plate-glass sides and ends. The roof was made as a louvred canopy, which could be opened to allow the bird song to be clearly heard. The bottom of the cage slid out like a drawer for cleaning. The door was circular, cut into the plate glass of the sides and moving on a pivoted steel hinge; even the drinking cup was of Waterford cut glass. Not surprisingly this elaborate piece of workmanship was costly—50 guineas—and had few if any imitators.

Attractive birdcages, with or without imitation occupants, have appealed to the rich as ornaments far back in history, especially perhaps in France. The inventory of Charles V of France, who died in 1380, mentions 'Cages of gold garnished with pearls, emeralds, sapphires and other precious stones'. Stuffed birds perfumed with exotic scents were apparently kept in them. Louis XI, who died in 1483, hung his salon with birdcages filled with glass lustres that made pleasant tinkling sounds.

Mechanical bird toys first appeared toward the end of the eighteenth century. Marie Antoinette owned a famous automaton in the form of a singing canary; but, not to be outdone, Catherine the Great of Russia commissioned a peacock in a cage musical box in 1780 from the famous clockmaker James Cox. Singing birds placed on top of musical snuffboxes were a favourite eighteenth-century conceit, and one of the triumphs of the Parisian manufacturer Jacquet Droz was a golden pistol toy, which, when the trigger was pressed, shot singing birds from its muzzle.

Napoleon presented Josephine with a life-size silver swan automaton, which is one of the most intricate of the surviving bird automata of the period. When the toy is set in motion, an ingenious system of fluted glass rods makes it look as though the water below the swan's body is rippling and silver fish, set beneath the glass, are moving through it. Meanwhile the swan itself performs a series of preening movements. The object was brought to England in the 1870s by the Bowes Lyon family, and Queen

Dutch blue and white pottery cage, c1750

Elizabeth the Queen Mother recalled it as one of the most fascinating ornaments of her childhood home. She did not, however, see it in its full glory of movement until 1963, when the oil-clogged working parts were cleaned and restored by London musical-box expert G. Sunley. The swan, now in the collection of the Bowes Museum, Barnard Castle, Yorkshire, was at the time of its restoration estimated to be worth about £10,000.

Originally singing-bird automata were craftsman-made toys for the wealthy, and could not be repeated; but during the 1820s and 1830s new techniques of production and new methods of organising labour enabled such items to be factory-made—almost mass-produced in fact, since the prefabrication assembly methods used were years ahead of their time— which brought singing-bird automata within the range of middle-class pockets. Movements for the automata at this stage were still the work of skilled watchmakers, and then as now the Swiss were reckoned to be the world best at the job. However, the manufacture of the wire cages and bases proved to be the kind of project that light engineering plants in the English Midlands could tackle economically, and in the Wolverhampton area several firms specialised in producing them. They were then shipped to Switzerland, where the mechanism and the bird figures were attached.

During the 1830s bird automata were close to the true musical box in design. A favourite type stood about 9 in high, the cage being of gilt and brass and the base usually of mahogany, so beloved by the English Regency manufacturer. Little attempt was made to reproduce a particular species of bird, it being enough that the songster was pretty and appealing. However, by the 1840s, when Edmund Perry and Henry Fearncombe had perfected a wire-drawing technique that spun the metal cage dome in a single operation, the ambition was to make the whole as authentic as possible. The birds, which by this stage were supplied usually by the English toymaking concern of Evans & Cartwright, were lifelike canaries or goldfinches.

The cages became bigger, too. They now had metal bases, usually of sheet iron, japanned and frequently embellished with swags or flowers and fruit in low relief. Initially either a single bird or a pair would be set

on a perch, perhaps with fake food vessels to heighten the illusion of reality, but as the Victorian age progressed it became the custom to include a clutter of scenic effects. Charles Bartems, who won a gold medal for his automata at the Paris exhibition of 1849, introduced birds under glass domes; and his prizewinning entry had stuffed humming birds on bocages (the potter's term for the leafy support work found on china statuettes) made of papier mâché with mirror-glass pools and a surround of seashells.

Although interest in the musical box as a drawing-room entertainment declined sharply toward the end of the nineteenth century—its relegation hastened by the invention of the phonograph—the mechanical bird automata were to persist in the form of coin-in-the-slot amusement machines on the English seaside pier throughout Edwardian times. Indeed this more innocent competitor of 'What the Butler Saw' was only stilled by the closure of the piers during the invasion scares early in World War II. After the war a more sophisticated taste made redundant even those bird machines that five years of rust and neglect had not rendered songless.

So the period 1750 to 1850 was one of the most fanciful for birdcage design. Elegance was vital to the well-to-do bird owner during this period, when Vanbrugh could be set to designing a dovecote (at Widdicombe Manor in Devon) or the Adam Brothers asked to turn their hand to manufacturing a combination clock and birdcage for the Duke of Northumberland (at Syon House, Middlesex). Though there is no record of the Chippendales designing birdcages, the Chippendale Chinese style had certainly found its way into birdcage design by Regency times, as did Strawberry Hill Gothic and, a little later, the Indian-inspired extravagances of the Brighton Pavilion, scaled down to birdcage proportions. George Durant even constructed an Egyptian 'hen-house' folly at Tong, Shropshire, between 1820 and 1840.

Roller canaries took Britain by storm in the 1820s. From the mid-eighteenth century, in fact, it had been common for a quantity of such songbirds to be hired out as an attraction at balls and assemblies. The

Singing automata of the early nineteenth century

*Coin-in-the-slot auto-
mata, early nineteenth
century*

Widdicombe Manor dovecote,
eighteenth century

cages would be grouped round the foot of a stairway, and at the entry
of the guest of honour the covers would be whipped away so that he was
greeted with a fanfare of birdsong. Alternatively, drawing or dining
rooms would be decorated with potted orange trees, with cages of canaries
and/or nightingales hung among the branches.

59

Chinese Chippendale-style birdcage and chair set

Quite a good living, by artisan standards, could be made from this kind of bird hire, as long as the birds would respond immediately to the light stimulus and sing on cue. Where normal roller training failed to achieve this response, however, some greedy owners, determined to make their birds sing as desired in the candlelit night, resorted to the cruel practice of blinding them with red-hot needles.

CHAPTER FOUR

The Rise of the Fancy

꽃꽃꽃꽃꽃꽃꽃꽃꽃꽃꽃꽃꽃꽃꽃꽃꽃꽃꽃꽃꽃꽃꽃꽃꽃꽃

The Industrial Revolution, materialistic but scientific, colours every aspect of life in the first half of the nineteenth century. Birds were not only considered pretty decorations for the salon, but also worth scientific study. When the London Zoo opened its doors to the public for the first time in 1828, they were already an important feature of the collection. In the previous year Decimus Burton had been commissioned to produce for the ravens an iron-framed aviary that is still renowned for its elegant design; though superseded by a more functional aviary, it now adorns the members' lawn as a monument of the early days of the Zoo. London's was the third great European zoo to be founded: Vienna Zoo was established in 1752 and Paris Zoo in 1793. In addition to the animals at the Paris Zoo, cranes dabbled in the stream and ostriches inhabited the area round the 'African Village' in the Jardin d'Acclimatation during the early nineteenth century. Next came zoos at Dublin in 1830, Amsterdam in 1837, Antwerp in 1841 and Stuttgart in 1842.

The nineteenth-century public was also prepared to pay handsomely to see a bird show. Wombell's Menageries, immortalised in the Staffordshire pottery ornaments of the 1820s, is clearly seen to have had several performing parrots, while one of the most successful travelling shows

Raven cage at London Zoo

Ostriches in the Jardin d'Acclimatation,
Paris

visiting London round that time contained performing canaries. Its two dozen performers included stars who simulated a roasting position by winding their legs round sticks; others walked the slack rope, wheeled each other about in barrows or played dead on command. Many of the troupe were attired in tiny uniforms consisting of soldiers' caps, swords and pouches. The attention aroused by this exhibition encouraged many imitators, and one of the most spectacular of the home-grown troupes was a party of goldfinches that paraded about with lighted tapers.

Another form of travelling bird show extremely popular during the first half of the nineteenth century was 'The Happy Family', in which a number of birds and animals, enemies in their natural state, were shown in a single cage. This show was the invention of John Austin, formerly a Nottingham stocking weaver, who had kept birds as a hobby but subsequently found that the antics of his pets could earn him more than his trade.

Austin and his family were summoned to give a command performance for Queen Victoria at Buckingham Palace in 1833. In his heyday he reckoned that he could take £1 a day at his regular pitch in the Waterloo

Regency birdcage

64

Road, London, but plagiaristic rivals and the changing tastes of a fickle public had reduced him to poverty when he died in the 1850s.

A typical Happy Family group and its owner were described by Mayhew in his *London Characters* of 1851. Mayhew's subject claimed to have been trained by Austin himself, and his group of assorted animals consisted of three cats, two dogs, two monkeys, two magpies, two jackdaws, two jays, ten starlings (some of which talked), six pigeons, two hawks, two chickens, one screech owl, five sewer rats, five white rats, eight guinea pigs, one wild and one tame rabbit, one hedgehog and one tortoise. The cost of feeding this mixed menagerie was around 12s a week.

Mayhew also interviewed a typical Victorian birdseller, who claimed to have been twenty-five years in the business. He sold 'larks, linnets and goldfinches to the captains of ships to take to the West Indies', and bought exotic birds from the sailors round Poplar and Limehouse for sale in the streets of London. Tastes in birds had changed vastly since he took up the business: as the century progressed customers had come to prefer the smaller types and birds such as jays, 'once the most popular' of his stock, were virtually unsaleable by the 1850s. His decision to become a birdseller had largely been forced upon him by his inability to take other work, being crippled from birth; but he enjoyed looking after birds and himself maintained a pet jackdaw.

Like small businessmen before and since he bemoaned his lack of capital to set himself up in quality birds and cages: 'I buy birds from different catchers,' he explained, adding that in times of his own financial hardship many of his suppliers had been good enough to give him credit. 'I haven't the money to buy the better kinds and I have to sell at 3d, 4d and 6d. If I had a pound to lay out for a few nice cages and good birds, I think I could do middling, especially in fine weather, for I'm a good judge of birds, and know how to manage them as well as anybody.' Buying cheap meant accepting large losses as a regular hazard of the trade, especially when dealing in linnets. 'I have had three parts of my linnets die, do what I might but not often so many. Then if they die all the food they have had is lost. There goes all for nothing the rape and flax seed for the linnets,

Porcelain cage of the 1820s

the canary and flax for the goldfinches, the chopped eggs for the nightingales and the German paste for the skylarks.' The birdseller's recipe for
German paste consisted of pea meal, treacle, hog's lard and moss seed.

In 1851 he reckoned that his bestselling line was goldfinches, adding
that when he was younger, he used to sell a lot of 'sparrows for shooting,
but that although he understood that sparrow shooting was still a fashionable sport, such birds were no longer in demand'. He considered that all
his customers were 'working people', in contrast to the Happy Family
proprietor, who found that his most generous patrons were drawn from
the middle classes.

It is not difficult to find a symbolic link between the nineteenth-century
artisan, cut off from his traditional rural environment by the Industrial
Revolution, and the caged linnet or goldfinch he kept as a pet. Equally
the bored daughters of the increasingly affluent English middle-class
household, whose family's desire for gentility denied them not only the
opportunity to work but any kind of social mobility, often found solace
in the company of imprisoned birds.

In earlier centuries bird fanciers had tended to be aristocrats, happy to
entrust the day-to-day care of the birds they maintained for aesthetic
pleasure or scientific study to a skilled employee, in just the same way
that the care of their liberty gamebirds was turned over to professional
gamekeepers, but for the new class of Victorian bird owners looking after
their birds was an enjoyable part of the hobby. The time the enthusiast
was able to lavish on his hobby in those more leisured days undoubtedly
accounted for much of his success in rearing 'difficult' cross-bred strains,
or keeping alive exotics in far from perfect conditions.

That cage birds were an integral part of English Victorian imagery and
experience can be judged by their frequent mention in music-hall songs.
Probably the most famous is the 'cock linnet' that accompanied Marie
Lloyd as she 'followed the van'. Although, strictly speaking, this song is of
twentieth-century origin, its elderly coster heroine, whose meagre
possessions are always on the move from lodging to lodging, is very much
a Victorian figure. 'Little Yellow Bird', a whimsical ditty recounting the

love of a sparrow for a caged canary, and 'A Bird in a Gilded Cage', a slightly naughty song comparing the situation of one of the more financially fortunate of the century's myriad 'fallen women' to that of a parlour pet, were both hit numbers in their day.

It was from the nineteenth-century artisan birdkeepers that the modern 'fancy' was to develop. Indeed it was in this period that fancying became the accepted technical term for the selective breeding of plants and animal species as a pastime.

Even in hobbies, however, the Victorian caste system was inescapable. Cavies (guinea pigs), fancy rabbits and fancy mice were bred enthusiastically by Victorian artisans, while in the years from 1820 to 1890 cottage gardeners took a special interest in growing pansies, pinks and auriculas of prize proportions. They also liked to encourage mutations and sports in these plants as the foundation of new strains, vividly, and sometimes to late twentieth-century eyes grotesquely, different from the norm. The equally enthusiastic middle class gardeners, on the other hand, concentrated their attention on ferns, orchids and pelargoniums.

Within the bird world a similar split occurred. Middle-class owners, whose primary interest was display, were attracted to the foreign finches, such as Java sparrows, and were quick to take advantage of novelties like the budgerigar. Artisan interest centred principally round permutations of the canary, though both groups shared an interest in native birds like the goldfinch, linnet and siskin. The first two were used by the artisan fancy to breed exhibition 'mules' or sterile hybrids for the show bench, and the last-mentioned used to breed some hardy varieties for their garden aviaries.

Although both groups were successful in breeding British species in captivity, the captive population was consistently supplemented by trapping, which was only finally outlawed by The Protection of Birds Act, 1954. However, from the end of the nineteenth century, when the first animal protection societies were founded and the conscience of the nation turned more and more to humane concern for all living creatures, there were opponents of trapping. Indeed, guilt about the trapping of

their pets and the more obvious cause of more entertainment outside the home may have helped in the levelling off and ultimate decline in popularity of birdkeeping by the end of the nineteenth century. Victorian birdkeeping was most popular in the 1860s, when it was estimated that at least 4,000 canary breeders in Norwich alone were engaged in supplying birds for the London markets.

From the 1840s onwards artisan canary owners began to organise themselves into clubs. The names selected, such as, in London, 'The Friendly' and 'The Hand in Hand', suggest that most clubs had a dual purpose—(1) for showing birds and exchanging information about stock management, and (2) as friendly societies. During this era trade unionism was illegal, and so the only way that working men could band together for mutual benefit or self-improvement was to form a society for members with a common hobby.

This serious aspect of the canary clubs is reflected in their rulebooks. For example, the code of the Derby Canary & Ornithological Society, founded in 1842, states: 'Any member who shall conduct himself in an unbecoming manner, or shall use intemperate language to a brother officer, or who shall smoke, or annoy any other member shall be fined 2s 6d or suspended from the society'.

An article on the London canary clubs appeared in the issue dated 12 December 1846 of the newly founded *Illustrated London News*. It laments the lack of written records among such societies, but suggests that some of the largest, such as the Royals, who met at the Grays Inn Coffee House, and the Friendly, who gathered at the British Coffee House in Cockspur Street, were already a century old. It was the usual practice for club show days, which were generally scheduled for late November or early December, to end with a grand banquet to which members' families and friends could be invited. The *Illustrated London News* report describes a typical banquet:

> The members and their guests are wont to assemble around a well-garnished table at five o'clock precisely. It is the custom of the chairman, after dinner, when the decanters have been placed before him, to call upon the first prize bird for a

ances of the new "Italian Opera" Company, were commenced immediately after the close of M. Jullien's term. The main object is to enlarge the horse-shoe Auditory, and augment the number of Boxes; and, at the same time, to increase the area of the Pit. On referring to Dibdin's plan, in Dibdin's "Edifices of the London Theatres," published in 1826, it will be seen that the Auditory does not occupy a sixth part of the entire plan: this, if we remember rightly, was partly owing to the increased number of private boxes, with their elegant ante-rooms, which encroachment upon the public boxes led to the memorable "O. P. row." However, considering the large, unappropriated, or useless space in the Theatre, there will be ample room for the new enterprise.

It is hard to follow histrionic changes in either of our Metropolitan Theatres. The roof illustration shows the interior of Covent Garden during the Far illuminations, yield the palm to the vast circle of Drury Lane. demolition, or rather the taking-down, of the Auditory: it is a sorry scene, as, indeed, an empty theatre is at any time. But here a host of workmen are disturbing the dust of thirty-seven years. The fronts of the boxes have nearly disappeared; and with them those finely-executed national emblems—the rose, shamrock, and thistle—fit ornaments for a Temple of the British Drama, once devoted to the ennobling art of a Kemble and a Siddons, now deserted by popular favour, and no longer available for the objects for which it was originally constructed.

Of the above, the following will be found correct. In Covent-Garden Theatre, there are, or rather were, seats for 2800 persons, exclusive of those in private boxes; but, on the visit of George IV., in 1823, 4255 persons paid for seats, exclusive of those in private boxes. Drury-Lane—"the wilderness," as Mrs. Siddons termed it—had seats for 3600 persons, though 5000 persons were occasionally wedged into the building. After Mr. Elliston had reduced the auditory, at an expense of £21,000, it held 3960 persons; but subsequent alterations must have reduced the number of seats. Covent Garden, from the front of the stage to the back of the pit, is 52ft. 9 in.; of the San Carlo, at Naples, 79 ft. 4¼ in.; of the Scala, at Milan, 77 ft. 5 in.; and of the Great Theatre at Parma, the largest in Europe, 152 ft. 7½ in.

ANNUAL SHOWS OF THE CANARY FANCY.

THE singular predilection which induce many ingenious gentlemen and others, to enroll themselves among the ranks of associated hobby riders, have each its various idiosyncrasy—

From grave to gay,
From lively to severe,

and each is pursued with a similar avidity to that which moved even the phlegmatic Dutchman during the well-known tulip mania in Holland.

LIZARD.—(No. 1.)

part of the head, which is covered by a patch of clear yellow. The back, which is marked with spangles in uniform stripes, corresponding with the trapezius, is an indication of the definitive state, the unsophisticated produce of nature being precise and geometrical.

The Canary known about twenty years ago as the "Spangled-back" (See Cut No. 2), will show the same process as that which appears in the Lizard, but much broken up, so evident is nature's consistency. It should be borne in mind as a beautiful truth, that there is an error on the part of the Fancy at that time.

Another notable consideration appears in the fact that the prize birds, previous to the first moulting, appear in a plumage nearly similar to that of the lizard, the only difference being in the lighter yellow marks of the young birds, the grey colour of the head is not so light, nor by a gloss of fine grey, similar to the effect of light upon an antique bronze. The legs of the prize bird, which were formerly black, are likewise represented by those of the lizard, these will continuing dark. This variety, which is not recognised by the Fancy, is a regular prize bird, is a favourite among the breeders of Nottingham, who are accustomed to produce some of the best specimens. It derives its name from the resemblance it bears to the colour and markings of the green lizard. From the above evidences, and the similarity which seems to exist between this bird and the description of the greenfinch, there is very little probability that any of the many varieties produced by cultivation, or by pairing with other tribes, that in this bird we may recognise the nearest approximation to the original species.

The Canary-finch is found in a wild state in the island of Madeira, where its

---

growing feather when in the blood, or while it performs a part in the circulation. This being done, the uniformity of black feathers continues uninterrupted.

In breeding the fancy birds great proficiency is shown in judicious pairing. A mealy bird and a jonquil being thus put together, the produce will not appear of the like qualities that parent birds; but the latter of the birds of such kind, mealy and jonquil. It is a curious fact that the mealy bird may be distinguished at an early age, by the invariable appearance of five feathers on the crest of the limb, which are not developed by the jonquil in any case.

The pious and excellent Dr. Watts has borne testimony to the harmony of the early condition of little birds. "Birds in their little nests agree," but it is not for the sake of veracity in this instance, that the worthy doctor stopped there; for he must have the young of the Canary scrambled from the procreant cradle ere they will fight like young harpies.

The above union, i.e. that of the mealy and the jonquil, is considered favourable to the production of pure birds; but if two strong birds are associated, the result will be an overcharge of colour in the next generation of birds. This appears, when the practice is continued, in a deterioration of the web of the feathers, which become frizzled and insufficient to cover the body, and the proper complement of tail and wing feathers will be wanting. A curious example of this is the habit of one correspondent. This shed upon the canary and to develop more than one single feather, the remainder of its body appearing like the scanty plumage of a Friesland hen. It was the habit of this odd bird to toy with the solitary feather which constituted its caudal appendage by drawing it through its beak, until it became quite curled up by such manipulation. This above proportion is not uncommon vice among better fledged birds; and it is the practice of attentive breeders to prevent it, by hanging a piece of string from the top of the cage, in order to divert the notice of the restless charge.

The Canary produces on an average four nests annually. The number of thirty-eight birds have been bred from two pair of birds during this year, and the produce of one cock and two hens has been known to amount to as many as forty; but these are not ordinary instances. However, the many casualties to which the birds are exposed renders advisable an extensive increase, so that the breeder is considered to do well who produces half a dozen male birds of each sort in the year.

The amount of prizes has varied at different times, and in different societies; it is governed by the number of the members. The prizes, which are ten in number, are given according to the price at which the bird, whether pale, mealy and jonquil. The two principal Shows are held in the last week in November and the first in December: the former, the Royals, at the Gray's Inn Coffee-house; and the latter, the Friendly, at the British Coffee-house, Cockspur-street; but are held at a variety of places, a numerous company, not supper in the presence of fair amateurs, assemble, to admire the tenants of the show cages.

And, as all associations would be incomplete without a concluding dinner, the members, with their friends and visitors, are wont to assemble round a well-garnished table of a friendly character. It is the custom of the Chairman, after dinner, when the decanters have been placed before him, to call upon the first prize bird for a song; which summons our feathered prodigy is generally terminated by an apology from the owner for the silence of his bird, and the voluntary offer, on his part, to perform as proxy. Many good songs, and good things too, follow

on the "Frilled" as follows:—" No bird shall be considered a fair show bird that has a feather or feathers without black, in stalk or web, in the flight or tail feathers; or that has less than eighteen flying feathers in each wing, and twelve in the tail.

Next to the perfection of the wings and tail—these being clearly defined by their black feathers forming a clear "saddle," or absolute separation of colour from the wing coverts—the qualities which entitle show birds to notice are as follows:—

The Jonquil (Cut No. 3), as its name denotes, is required to be of a pure deep yellow, entirely free from any green tinge; the colour is deeper on the cap, over the edge. In both of these varieties the purity of development will be discovered, but such a quality is not recognised by the judges.

In the mealy-bird (Cut No. 4) the golden plumage of back, breast, and head, appears frosted over, or powdered, through the small feathers producing a whitish edge. In each case this price is obtained by the bird whose colour is most perfect, and that at the same time shows the result of high breeding; it will be discovered, but such a quality is not recognised by the judges.

After the second moult, the Canary is no longer a show bird, the dark feathers in the wings and tail then disappearing entirely.

The mealy-bird, as it has already been stated, similar to the appearance of the lizard. The Canary is then in its most perfect state as a fancy bird, and it loses the distinction immediately after.

Among other points of nice attention which are required during the moult, it is necessary to observe if any of the quill feathers are accidentally or prematurely shed (beaten out), in which case they would be reproduced colourless, or "foul," to provide against this, it is the practice of breeders to extract the

SPANGLED-BACK.—(No. 2.)

Rabbits, bantams, pigeons, "little dogs and all," have their especial votaries in numerous sections of the general body denominated the "Fancy," whose prodidents do not fail to discover in objects that, to the uninitiated, would appear o little import, a significance which practically refutes the time-honoured proverb, familiarity breeds contempt."

The celebrated Linnæus could not find matter for the contemplation of a lifetime in the humblest of all which a clown would tread unconsciously beneath his feet.

There are few things so minute or insignificant, but that a diligent observation of their peculiarities may serve to reveal a degree of comparative interest which appertain to them as indispensable links in the great chain of creation.

We are taught that the wisest of men was acquainted with all things, "from the cedar of Lebanon even to the hyssop on the wall," and was admonished by his example not to despise or overlook the small works of nature.

Moreover, it is good for a man to ride his hobby; for are we so perfect, or so dull, as not to possess some superfluous activity over and above the animus necessary for the common duties and the considerate use of whatever wholesome objects of life, and it is well that such an elegant should effervesce upon some object at once inexpensive and without offence.

Among the members of the Fancy, the societies for improving the breed of the Canary birds constitute a great acquisition, and are denominated the Friendly, the Royals, the Amateurs, and the Hand in Hand.

It is to be regretted that such societies and their predecessors have not preserved any connected record of their transactions, together with some account of their other aims; in the progressive changes which their exertions have effected on the appearance of the bird. It would appear that such societies have existed for upwards of a century, but, in the absence of any memorial of the earlier days of the Fancy, tradition fails to make us acquainted with any particulars of its origin and progress, or with the sources whence the original stock was obtained.

The first introduction of the Canary-finch into Europe appears to have occurred in the fourteenth century, or soon after the discovery of the Canary Islands, when it is said to have been conveyed to the mother-country by the Spanish colonists. He was the original property of the Spaniards, who were incapable of some centuries later. Bechstein, a German author, states that in the beginning of the sixteenth century, a vessel containing a portion of these birds, destined for Leghorn, was wrecked on the coast of Italy, opposite to the island of Elba, where, on being set at liberty, birds sought the nearest land, which was the isle of Elba, and soon became a favourite with the bird-fanciers, the birds increased, circumstance of note but male birds having been thus conveyed, it is no uncommon...

The male and female propagate equally with those of the male or female Canaries, and the Regular Prize Canary, being of a greenish bronze throughout, excepting the upper

*Flachsen Grummaporat (Canary Grass), an annual grass, cultivated for its seeds, which the common food of the Canary. It is now produced abundantly in Kent.

MEALY-BIRD.—(No. 4.)

and the annual labours and triumph of the Canary Fancy conclude under the genial influence of good cheer, and amid the conciliating interchange of mutual sentiments.

[The specimens of the mealy bird and the jonquil, in the above cuts, were drawn from first prize birds, both the property of the same breeder.]

THE THEATRES.

We must not look for any very great novelty in the theatrical world until Christmas. All the department's energies are just now in full activity, preparing for the Christmas, which will form the chief entertainment. Indeed, we believe the Haymarket is the only house that will put forward a burlesque. There is something curious in this change of managerial opinion. Last winter it was supposed that nothing would attract but a fairy tale. This year we find the latter again in the ascendant, the burlesques having been fairly run to death. There have been plenty of topics during the last six months to joke upon, mechanically or otherwise. Pantomimes will, however, be as popular until the story and fatigue of the opening is made, in some measure to run through the entire piece.

HAYMARKET.

On Monday evening, an actress new to the Perfection. She was called at this theatre, as Kate Reynolds, from the American theatres," but we heard in this theatre that she was English by birth. However, this is of little consequence; we have only to record the success of her début, which was complete and most satisfactory. Miss Reynolds appears to us to be a great acquisition to our stage speak of the theatres generally, as, in the Haymarket, Miss P. Horton would have played the character equally well; but Miss Reynolds having been eminently calculated to perform any character in a line of all others most difficult to fill—that which, we think, on the French stage, is termed that of soubrette—a line which is little superior to the "singing chambermaid" of our English dramatic distinctions. The new actress is a perfect mistress of her art; she has a lee speaking voice, and an exceedingly pretty face; she is not actressy at all, and her acting a perfect ease. "She is of good height," and "The Gondolette," she was loudly and generally encored; and all through the piece the most flattering demonstrations of the approval of the audience greeted her. At the conclusion, she was unanimously called for, and received the customary tribute, in a most graceful acknowledgement. The other characters were very badly played by Messrs. Tilbury, Holl, and Clark, and Mrs. Humby. The scene between the two latter performers was acted to the life; but, where have we a lady's maid like that which Mrs. Humby can proper salary; otherwise, we think, any "fast" man-about-town would settle any liberal annuity upon him, were it only to ride, either behind him or his cab. On Wednesday evening, a curious circumstance occurred. A new farce, called "Story Telling," was amongst the attractions of the evening; and it had percocked but a few minutes, when Mr. Farren, who was playing in it, came forward, and said that, farce being incapable of giving proper effect, he was obliged to ask indulgence of the audience, and after a short lapse of time, the drama of "Suzanne" was proceeded with.

SALE OF AN ALLEGED AUTOGRAPH OF SHAKSPEARE.—On Monday, a sale by auction of a curious collection of old plays, &c., took place at Messrs. Puttick and Simpson's rooms, and amongst them some manuscript notes and a signature, presumed to be the autograph of William Shakspeare. These were "catalogued as volume of a Shakspeare's (first edition, 1877, imperfect. The auctioneer stated that he would not guarantee the signature to be genuine, but that it, as well as the manuscript notes, were presumed to be in the autograph of the "immortal bard." There was but one offer made for this volume, viz., £5, at which sum it was knocked down to a gentleman named Holding.

song, which summons not being responded to by the feathered bi-ped, some little pause ensues.

This interruption is generally terminated by an apology from the owner for the silence of his bird, and the voluntary offer on his part to perform as proxy. Many goods and good things follow and the annual labours and triumphs of the canary fancy conclude under the animating influence of good cheer and amid conciliating interchange of mutual sentiment.

Although the prizes at such shows could be the now traditional cups and rosettes, often the winner received household goods instead. These were presumably acceptable not only because the early canary-club members were drawn from the steadfastly respectable semi-skilled or craftsman classes, but also because this sort of prize went a long way towards placating wives for the time that husbands lavished on their birds.

The practice continued at some clubs well into the 1860s. Thus a schedule for a show given by the Leigh Canary Fanciers in 1869 reads: 'Prizes £12 in value; 13 copper kettles, 9 teapots, 6 coffee pots, 7 cruet stands, table and teaspoons, timepiece, cutlery, six sets of carvers, boots and pipes, the whole presenting a pretty and useful appearance'.

One of the commercial centres for pet birds in Victorian London was Sclater Street, probably better known by the name of the market which still meets there each Sunday—Club Row. This bisected a working-class district known as The Nichol and was its social centre. In the seventeenth century this area had housed refugee Huguenot silk weavers, and it is probable that the association of the market with pet birds derives directly from their interest in the hobby.

By the 1850s, however, the district had degenerated into one of the worst slums in London. It was a meeting ground not only for legitimate traders but for the local criminal community, and often the two interests converged in the selling of livestock that in no way conformed to the pedigree claimed for it. The unsuspecting purchaser could be badly swindled, and the legend grew among Londoners that any canary bought in Club Row only needed a bath to reveal itself as a sparrow covered with yellow paint.

Generally speaking, however, the canaries that most interested the London fanciers were not clear yellows but the brokenly marked 'spangles' or the yellow-capped brown or green ticked types now designated 'lizards'. The 'London Fancy' last seems to have been common in the early 1900s and a call to fanciers holding stocks between the wars to make a real effort to revive the breed failed to produce any response. It was officially declared extinct by the governing bodies of the fancy in 1945.

A strong canary fancy existed among the miners of the Scottish lowlands and the Yorkshire coalfields during the nineteenth century. Their birds accompanied them down the pits to act as an early warning system against the perils of firedamp; this practice continued into the early 1950s, when more scientific methods made it obsolete. Curiously enough, one of the schemes to boost coal output in Scotland during World War II was the establishment of a rescue station in the Coatbridge area, one of whose duties was to increase the distribution of canaries to the nearby pits. The station aimed at supplying two canaries for every 100 miners in the district. It also devised a special respiratory cage topped with a miniature oxygen cylinder, so that at the first signs of distress the oxygen flow could be turned up and the bird revived to return to safety with its master.

The Yorkshire fancy developed a tall thin strain of canary which even today rates as Britain's second most popular breed; and in Scotland breeders created the quaintly shaped 'Scots Fancy', which carried its head at an angle lower than its shoulders. A similar shape of bird was developed by the miner fanciers of the Belgian coalfields and is still popular on the Continent today. In Britain, however, changing tastes have made unnaturally shaped canaries very much a minority interest.

There was also a very strong nineteenth-century canary fancy in the Lancashire cotton towns, where the Lancashire coppy or curly feathered canary was a favourite. A very clear picture of the activities of Manchester canary breeders of the 1860s has been left for posterity by the Rev Francis Smith, curate of St Paul's, Manchester, from 1850 to 1864, and later rector of Moorby, near Boston, in Lincolnshire. He first became interested in canaries when he bought one as a pet for his daughter Judy.

Like most Victorian writers on birds, his approach is chatty and his text based on not always accurately observed personal experience. Somewhat surprisingly for a mid-Victorian cleric he is far less inhibited in his treatment of mating than, for example, William Edwin Baxter, author of *The Feathered Vocalist*, published in 1830, who wrote in his foreword that he had 'attempted to divest the contents of any terms which might be considered ungrateful to the ear of modesty, or unassociated with the language of feminine delicacy, yet at the same time making the subject interesting to those who feel pleasure in becoming the fostering guardians of incarcerated minstrels'.

What Francis Smith found shocking about the canary trade of his time was the way in which this hobby had become almost a mania with some who could scarcely afford it. He writes in *The Canary* published in 1869:

> The breeding of canaries by the working classes in the manufacturing districts is not only a favourite pursuit but a profitable trade.
>
> The numbers which they annually breed, and the prices which they give for a good canary, will appear fabulous and altogether unjustifiable to those unacquainted with the subject. Our artisans in Manchester think nothing of giving one, two and three pounds for a single bird.
>
> On a Saturday afternoon and night the market and shops—as well as the public houses used for the purpose—are crowded with men and lads, having either birds to sell or looking on and watching what goes on around them.
>
> The veriest tyro in the business thinks as little of giving five or ten shillings for a bird as he does of giving eightpence for a pound of steak to frizzle with his tea, and the prices that they will give for a *good* canary will appear fabulous to those unacquainted with the subject. As much as £25 has been recorded for a single specimen of exceptionally high quality Belgian stock.

Obviously such trading was prey to sudden changes in local prosperity, such as the depression caused by the cotton famine during the American Civil War, when Mr Smith noted the sad spectacle of one-time flourishing fanciers selling off first their birds, and finally their cages, in order to obtain food for their families.

While praising the pursuit of birdkeeping as 'a vast step in the way of civilisation, and infinitely in advance of the cockfighting and bull-baiting of former days', Mr Smith cannot approve the frequent association of drinking with birdkeeping, a feature of the Manchester show schedule in the 1860s:

> For lack of support by the upper classes of society, and for want of a suitable room elsewhere, I am sorry to say that meetings are held chiefly at some tavern, whose landlord finds it in his interest to give a considerable sum (around £5) in order that the meetings be held in his house.
>
> I have before me now a bill announcing a grand annual show of Belgian canaries which was to take place last Whit Saturday at a certain public house in this town whose landlord offers £4 10s on the condition that the show is held at his house, that he have the appointment of the judges, that the birds shown remain for exhibition until the night following the day of the show, which of course is Sunday, and that every member spends 6d each monthly meeting night, which I am sorry to add is also Sunday.

Aviculture could be expensive, and sometimes ruinous—not only for

Early nineteenth-century designs for garden aviaries

artisan fanciers, but also for the genteel readers of Mr Shirley Hibberd's *Rustic Adornments for the Home of Taste*, first published in 1857:

> Aviaries are expensive luxuries and those who contemplate adding one to the number of their recreative resources are earnestly advised to first count the cost. . . .
> We are disposed to advise our readers to begin birdkeeping with moderate ambition, and at every enlargement of the pastime to take heed that it does not overpass reasonable limits. One bird lovingly cared for as a member of the family is of far more real value to enliven the household than any number, however rare and costly, that entail more trouble than can be endured to do thorough justice to them.

The garden aviary was the particular delight of the middle-class Victorian birdkeeper, who copied in miniature the elaborate garden aviaries of eighteenth-century stately homes. Shirley Hibberd himself suggests Moorish palaces for parrot cages and intricate Chinese constructions for canaries, and although he warns, in discussing birdcage design, that 'a mistake may very easily be made in the desire to secure something pretty—and in truth a considerable number of the fancy cages displayed for sale in the shops are unfit for any useful purpose', he states elsewhere that 'elegant birds deserve elegant cages', and is not above illustrating his articles with such excrescences of taste as a combination birdcage and goldfish bowl (see page 126).

In the Victorian passion for ornament, commonsense was often ignored. Take, for example, the sad case of William Kidd, of Ravenscourt Park, near London, who wrote to the *Gardeners' Chronicle* in January 1850 to bemoan the reduction of what had been a collection of more than 300 birds—'one at least for every day of the year'—to a mere eleven specimens. 'I built my birds a large and commodious aviary fitted in style worthy of its inhabitants, the agreemens (*sic*) of well-polished looking and toilet glasses, everlasting fountains and leafy foliage not being wanting to render their house an ornithological palace.' He had, however, omitted to

A page from a mid-Victorian birdcage-dealer's catalogue

make the structure rat-proof, and, after losing most of his birds, had to transfer the remainder to cages and turn the original building into a greenhouse.

The Victorian middle class turned for practical advice on birdkeeping to the gardening press. A contributor to the *Gardeners' Chronicle* of January 1843 wrote:

> The addition of an aviary to the amateur's garden increases the pleasure of horticultural labour, gives cheerfulness to the scene and well repays any attention to the comforts of the little songsters.
> What can be more joyous than the early carol of the canary and the goldfinch on a bright spring morning?
> Even in winter, the sharp chirp and quaint notes of the chaffinch and bullfinch are quite delightful. The facility with which these birds can be preserved through the winter in the open air, the simplicity and cheapness of their food makes it desirable that no pleasure ground or garden should be without an aviary.

The feature provides do-it-yourself instructions for aviary building, though the accommodation is cramped by modern standards and would certainly restrict breeding:

> Any snug corner facing south or south by east is favourable. A bird house 8 ft x 4 ft 8 in high is sufficient for forty or fifty inhabitants.
> The aviary roof should be conical, as it provides a warmer roosting place at night than a flat one. The back and sides of the aviary should be built up and the front divided into two compartments each covered with neat wirework to keep out mice.

Elsewhere the writer recommends canaries, bullfinches, chaffinches, redpoles and Java sparrows as suitable for beginners. Numerous other birds were also recommended by other writers. For example, the Loudons, in their extremely successful volume *The Villa Gardener*, published in 1850, talk of silver and gold pheasants, partridges, quail, red, black and wood grouse, pigeons, turtle doves, Muscovy ducks, Canadian geese, bustards, gulls and 'curious varieties of fowl' such as bantams, all being suitable for aviaries in the neighbourhood of London.

They considered the ideal aviary to be a 'small rustic structure with an enclosed court covered with netting', but also listed more ambitious bird houses, which the enthusiast might like to copy. For them the 'handsomest' aviaries in England in 1850 were those at Woburn Abbey in Bedfordshire and at Cobham Hall in Kent. There was formerly a tolerably complete aviary at the Duke of Devonshire's villa at Chiswick (see page 49), but it had been given up about 1840; and the most complete aviary for singing birds was at Knowsley Hall near Liverpool.

The Loudons' life's work was *Cottage, Farm and Villa Architecture*, which provides instructions for producing everything from a gothic folly for the garden to a working water-closet in the house, and when the widowed Jane Loudon revised it about 1857, she added more detail to the section on aviary building.

> Aviaries are of two kinds. Those for birds of song and those for birds of show. The former are not very common in Britain but where they do exist they are usually joined to conservatories.

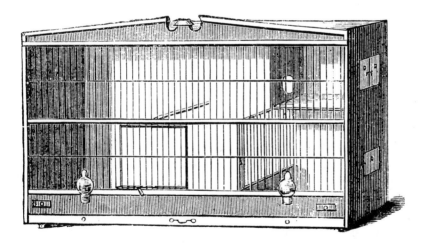

The old 'London' type of breeding cage, reproduced from Wallace's The Canary Book

Their general form and style should harmonise with those of the house. No particular shape or dimensions are requisite, but it is always desirable to have the whole or a part of the roof of glass, to have glass windows on at least two sides and to have a complete lining of wirework within every window and door to prevent the escape of the birds, and the ingress of vermin when the sashes are opened for ventilation.

There should also be a porch with double doors for the same purpose.

Some aviaries are formed on a large scale and include trees, shrubs and turf, the whole being covered with wire netting.

In this case, the extent ought to be considerable and the birds few, otherwise the trees and shrubs will soon be injured and the whole rendered unsightly.

One feels that Mrs Loudon herself is not keen on birds and has only added to the section on aviaries because of their popularity among her readers. The chapter continues:

When the object is simply to hear the song of birds, it is found a more cleanly and effective plan to distribute a few cages up and down a conservatory or along a veranda. The birds sing better when they are within hearing, but not within sight of each other and the cages prevent that appearance of dirt on the trees, plants and paths which is generally offensive in a crowded aviary.

To prevent the possibility of any dirt, seeds, etc., being thrown down from the birds in cages, the latter may be constructed with a small cellar or box from 4 in to 8 in deep in the bottom in which alone food and water may be placed, the bird descending through an opening in the upper floor to eat his food and ascending by a small ladder or stair.

In recommending this two-tier bird house Mrs Loudon may well have been recalling some of the cages she had seen on display in Victorian ironmongers or pet shops, for by the 1850s the majority of bird owners bought their cages. A trade catalogue of the 1850s, now in the British Museum, shows cages styled like dolls' houses, Swiss chalets complete with toy stags' heads and antlers over the door, and Eastern temples adorned with minarets.

For the middle-class parlour the wire-all-round display cage was favoured, but the artisan intent on breeding tended to prefer the box cage with closed back and sides. It was within the 'fancy', therefore, that the elegant lines of Regency cage design lingered longest: for instance, the

Palmers pet store, Sclater Street, London, 1880

'London style' breeding cage advocated by Wallace in his *Canary Book* in 1875, and one of the most popular items stocked by Palmers Pet Store of Sclater Street when it opened in 1880 retains the classical decoration of a broken pediment above the wire front.

Conservatories flourished in Victorian gardens. Tropical birds plus 'rockwork, statuary, fountains and a tree top level walk' were among the attractions of the mighty Chatsworth conservatory, completed in 1843 for the Duke of Devonshire, and so large that Queen Victoria drove through it in a pony chaise. It attracted so much public interest on open days—48,000 visitors on one day—that a special railway station had to be opened in the vicinity. Many who saw it were eager for something similar, though on a smaller scale, and 'Paxton's patent' combination conservatory/greenhouse and tropical bird house was advertised in the gardening press of the 1880s to supply this demand.

Parrots and parakeets were popular inmates for such conservatories. The budgerigar, which belongs to the parakeet family, first occurs in a list of antipodean fauna, 1794. One of the first to import one into Britain was John Gould, whose *Handbook to the Birds of Australia* was published in 1840. He soon fell under the spell of the 'budgie' and wrote:

> As cagebirds they are as interesting as could possibly be imagined. For independent of their highly ornamental appearance, they are constantly coquetting, squabbling and assuming every variety of graceful posture.
>
> Indeed I am unacquainted with any Australian species brought to England which has contributed so much to the pleasure of those who keep living birds.

Breeding cage

Early budgerigar imports were expensive, fetching up to £25 a pair, but by 1859 50,000 a year were being imported and their price dropped accordingly. One ship alone carried 4,000 pairs and a single dealer sold 15,000 pairs in four months. It was usual for the trade to pay 2s a bird, of which the sailor who had cared for the livestock en route got 1s.

The birds were generally well fed during the trip, since they represented a considerable profit if they arrived safe and sound, but, surprisingly, they were never given water.

By the 1860s we find a writer recalling:

> It seems but only yesterday we thought ourselves fortunate to obtain a pair for five guineas, although now we may expect to see hundreds of them hawked about the streets on costermongers' barrows for a few shillings the pair . . . They play like mice about the cage and chirrup the while like very loud sparrows.

In the 1860s, as now, budgerigars (then called lovebirds), seem to have been slippery customers, for the same writer ends with a warning: 'while these birds are fast becoming acclimatised, we must not be misled by reports of the appearance of flocks of them in company with the sparrows in the Temple Gardens'.

Strangely enough, the London Zoo did not acquire its first budgerigar until 1862.

The first budgerigars to be bred successfully by a German fancier were hatched in 1855, but generally speaking the Germans stayed faithful to the canary, treating the budgerigar as a novelty only.

All the early budgerigars had the green/yellow colouration natural to wildlings, the first colour break achieved by selective breeding being an all-yellow bird in 1884. It was not until 1900 that Dutch breeders achieved the production of a pale grey-headed bird, which was the first step on the road to sky blue shades.

From this point on, breeders tried to develop pastel-shaded budgerigars. The first true skys were exhibited by Mr Sutton at the Horticultural Hall, London, in 1910, and the first white British budgerigars, true to type and not accidental albino individuals, were shown in 1922 by Tom Goodwin.

Returning to the pages of the *Gardeners' Chronicle* for the 1860s, we find their bird expert recommending 'a cage of waxbills and avadavats as one of the best drawing room ornaments', and describing them as 'angels that have lost their wings—no, not lost their wings, merely their heavenly state and immunity from death. A cageful of them will assuredly suggest a lot of cupids in a crate'. The fecundity of these little birds suggests that not all Victorian children remained ignorant about the habits of the birds and bees, and that, then as now, the possession of a pair of pets was for parents the easy way round the more awkward inquiries of the sexually curious young.

In those earnest times many middle-class mid-Victorian families felt it insufficient that birdkeeping was enjoyable in its own right. The pursuit had to be publicly justified as a part of the moral education of the nursery-bound youngster. Thus Shirley Hibberd can talk of 'birds which are petty tyrants and need to be put into solitary confinement until they expiate their crimes'. He adds for the further benefit of parents:

A breeding cage inhabited by a faithful pair of canaries is as good a household toy as will be found amongst a thousand.

The interest that young people take in their welfare should commend such a toy to the domestic circle, and the stern utilitarian may see in it an instrument in the air of education.

The introduction to the fireside of a lively scrap from the book of nature is something which better lessons may be learned than from the best of Latin grammars or solemn treatises of physical education.

꒜꒜꒜꒜꒜꒜꒜꒜꒜꒜꒜꒜꒜꒜꒜꒜꒜꒜꒜꒜꒜꒜꒜꒜꒜꒜꒜꒜

CHAPTER FIVE

The Budgerigar (Parakeet) Boom

꒜꒜꒜꒜꒜꒜꒜꒜꒜꒜꒜꒜꒜꒜꒜꒜꒜꒜꒜꒜꒜꒜꒜꒜꒜꒜꒜꒜

The break-up of the settled hierarchy of the nineteenth century through increased political awareness among the artisan and middle classes, and almost frenzied frivolity in an English aristocracy freed from the yoke of Victorianism, discouraged home-based hobbies. Aviculture boasted plenty of solid adherents, who, it could be said, were keeping more birds better than ever before, but it was no longer fashionable. This decline in fashion had begun in late Victorian times, for whereas the early editions of *Rustic Adornments for the Home of Taste* carried extensive notes on birdkeeping, the 1870 edition replaced them by instructions on how to organise a marine aquarium.

One attempt to give aviculture a firmer base was the founding of the Avicultural Society in 1894; it was the first society of its type in the world, and is still flourishing. Avicultural societies were formed in America in 1927 and in Australia in 1928.

From 1890 to World War I birdkeeping revolved round the show circuit, which in England largely meant the 'National' shows held at the Crystal Palace, London. Such events were not only the shop window of the fancy but its most important bloodstock mart. Inferior birds were given classes of their own, a condition of entry being that every bird

Drawing of an old-time bird-room from Blakston's Book of Canaries and Cage Birds

shown would be available for purchase after judging. These classes attracted entries of anything up to 500 birds a time; in Manchester, mecca of the northern fancy, shows held at Belle Vue were considered to be poor if there were less than 1,000 birds tabled.

Show news was the main information given in the fast-proliferating specialist press, though features on cage-bird management still occasionally appeared in journals for artisans, such as the monthly *Illustrations*. The 1890s, however, was the epoch when periodicals like *Fur and Feather—incorporating Small Pets* were being launched. *Cage Birds*, now the most important of the British aviculture journals, first appeared in 1900. A penny a copy was the usual price for the commercial cage-bird publications.

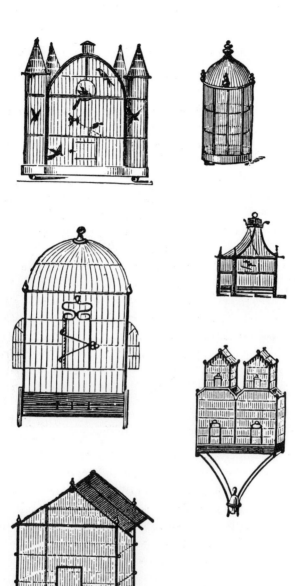

Page from a French bird-cage manufacturer's trade catalogue, 1890s

Study of the specialist press of the 1890s seems to indicate that some kind of epidemic swept through British aviaries and birdrooms at the time, decimating the birds to the point of putting many fanciers out of the hobby for good. Its exact nature is difficult to diagnose, for fanciers seem to have been reluctant to admit that any bird of theirs was ever even 'seedy'. Nevertheless, a preoccupation with bird health is characteristic of this decade.

It is, of course, highly probable that fanciers were paying for the enormous bird boom of the mid-century. Then, the widespread demand for cheap pets, and breeding to fix show characteristics thought desirable in strains that were in any case—as with the curly feathered or hunch-backed canaries—based on a natural deformity, had weakened the general health and stamina of birds so much that their resistance to quite minor ailments was virtually nil. This situation might have been repeated with the budgie boom of 1955-65, but for the much improved scientific knowledge of modern fanciers. Quite complex genetic patterning, and dietary systems based on a knowledge of vitamin and general nutritional requirements, can give the effects desired without unwanted side-effects.

Turning from disease to more frivolous matters, the early bird journals offered their readers plenty of odd gadgets and eccentric advice. Typical is an Edwardian advertisement for 'The Demon Smasher'—a cast-iron contraption priced at 3s and designed to convert 'ordinary or garden pebbles into grit for cage-bird consumption'. And 'Cross' the 'Wild beast king of Liverpool', suggested that the best way for aviary owners to tackle the problem of rats was by getting a mongoose! The price of this 'aid no bird man should be without' was, however, not specified.

As for prices, *Cage Birds* quotes Norwich canaries—not show champions certainly but birds of 'reasonable quality'—in its early issues at 7s 6d each for cocks and, according to age, 3s to 5s for hens.

The principal preoccupation of the fancy from 1900 was colour. Although some white canaries seem to have been successfully reared in Europe in the late seventeenth and early eighteenth centuries, the secret was lost—or more possibly brushed aside—by the Victorian preoccupation

Modern German-made birdcage, constructed in the manner popular in the early 1900s

with spangled plumage. So research had to begin again, until, in 1908, a snow white specimen was exhibited at a London show.

German fanciers, too, were much taken with the idea of white canaries, and succeeded in producing and marketing them internationally. Until the outbreak of World War I brought the trade to a close, the price in London for a Munich-reared white canary was £5.

There was also widespread interest in the possibility of breeding a scarlet canary without recourse to colour feeding. It had long been known that by mixing substances such as red pepper with a canary's food its feathers could be temporarily tinted, but of course the moment these feathers were lost in the moult the bird reverted to its natural shade. Success in breeding in the red, however, did not come till later (see page 98).

Certain sections of the canary fancy were attempting miniaturisation. Border canaries were already colloquially known as Wee Gems, and in the USA this description is perhaps more widely recognised as a technical term than the correct one. Today's Border canary breeders insist that the neat format of *their* canary is the closest approximation in domesticated and improved form to the original canary finch.

The Border was first noted as a distinctive breed around 1826. It was then the variety most widely kept by the shoemakers and weavers of the Anglo-Scottish border towns, and it is said that the Border first arrived in England when a Langholm Scottish shoemaker moved house to Cumberland. Much of the development of the strain took place in Cumberland, and at the formation of the original Border Fancy Club in 1890 there was a strong faction which wanted to call the bird Cumberland Fancy. The original club membership was forty-three breeders, but by 1955 the total had reached nearly 1,000, quite apart from the Border owners who regarded their birds solely as pets. Modern show-standard Border canaries must measure not more than $5\frac{1}{2}$ inches from beak-tip to tail-tip; this compares with the 1970s show standard for Yorkshires of $6\frac{3}{4}$ inches, though in the past, when sheer length was the aim of many enthusiasts for this strain, birds of up to 9 inches were not uncommon.

Victorian birdcage

92

By crossing the Border canary with the crested roller, breeders evolved a new strain, subsequently called the Gloster, which made its debut in 1925. Glosters were to remain very much a specialist fancier's choice for their first fifteen years of existence in Britain, and even the record-breaking 'National' show of 1940 could produce only twenty-six Gloster cocks and fourteen hens. The Gloster was, however, from the first a canary that appealed to the American market, and the American 'fancy' greatly improved the strain during World War II.

Large late Victorian aviaries are few, but one of the finest examples, in cast-iron, built at Waddesdon Manor, Buckinghamshire, in the 1880s, is still used for its original purpose of housing pheasants—the grounds also house a flock of free-flying macaws. Its special attraction is the way in which it is placed in its setting—a formal garden, bounded by a hornbeam hedge and having a large lawn flanked by borders of 'Iceberg' roses. The garden is further ornamented with marble statuary and metal birds. The aviary itself is rococo in style, perhaps copied from an eighteenth-century original, and was probably built under the direction of the distinguished French architect G. H. Destailleur, who was also responsible for designing the Manor House, built around the same time. There is some evidence that the aviary was prefabricated in Belgium and shipped to Waddesdon in sections for erection.

One landowner who did continue in the tradition of the eighteenth-century gentleman scientists was, of course, the Duke of Bedford, father of the present Duke, who established at Woburn Abbey Britain's first flock of homing budgerigars, and wrote what was to become a standard work on members of the parrot family.

During the early twentieth century there was a considerable growth of interest in parrot keeping. At the more humble level this may have been due to soldiers importing 'African greys' after the Boer War, but there was also interest in the royal household. Coco, an African grey with a vocabulary that included 'God Save the Queen', which it had been taught by the royal children to greet their grandmother, Queen Victoria, was a favourite at Sandringham.

Lord Snowdon's 'Romantic Gothic' aviary; its prototype is owned by England's Queen Mother and filled with budgerigars

This early experience of birdkeeping probably gave George V his lifelong passion for budgerigars. Among his collection at Sandringham in the 1920s was a rare strain of Australian Blues. The King agreed in 1930 to become patron of the Budgerigar Society, an act which set an official seal of superiority on budgerigar-keeping! Queen Elizabeth the Queen Mother has carried on the tradition by maintaining in her private gardens at Windsor a flock of multi-coloured homing budgerigars; it was for these birds that Lord Snowdon originally designed his 'Romantic Gothic' aviary, subsequently manufactured and marketed commercially.

Another famous budgerigar enthusiast was the conductor, the late Sir Malcolm Sargent, whose pet would perch on his baton as he rehearsed and sip from his wine glass at dinner. Budgerigars who enjoyed a nip of their owner's tipple were also kept in his declining years by Sir Winston Churchill; the most famous of these was Toby, who shared a liking for whisky and soda, and would zoom about the Cabinet Room during Sir Winston's last years in office. When Toby eventually escaped, in Monte Carlo, Sir Winston was presented with a replacement by Aristotle Onassis, but as far as its owner was concerned this bird was not a success— it bit. Possibly Mr Onassis had not taken sufficient trouble to ascertain the sex of the bird he bought: although the two sexes will learn to perform tricks or to mimic the human voice equally well, the hens who in the wild have to chew wood to make nests, have more tendency to nip— indeed, in captivity they will indulge in bouts of destructiveness when in peak breeding condition.

The budgerigars widely kept in garden aviaries during the 1930s were halfway between the original wild parakeet of Australia and the modern cage bird. The final transformation to the modern bird was to be achieved during World War II—a watershed in the history of bird-keeping. A glance through the specialist press of the period would suggest that the fancy was little affected by the war; the mood, as fanciers prepared for the 1940 'National', held in London's Horticultural Hall since the destruction of the Crystal Palace by fire in 1936, was one of buoyant optimism. Profits from the event were to be given to the Red Cross, and patriotism boosted entries to a record-breaking 5,040. Wartime restrictions on travel, which made any kind of nearby entertainment popular with Londoners, also made this a record show for visitors, both fanciers and the general public. A star exhibit was a patriotic mynah whose owner had taught it to mimic the 'Jairmany Calling' call-sign of the broadcaster of pro-German propaganda known to derisive British radio listeners as Lord Haw-Haw.

Yet after the Indian summer of 1940 the fancy was not to be quite the same again. The hint of hard times ahead could be gleaned from the changing tenor of the classified advertisements in the specialist journals: aviaries and livestock were suddenly being offered at bargain rates, as manufacturers and breeders closed down for the war's duration; customers were not necessarily plentiful, for bird seed became more and more difficult to obtain, and—as judges and showring personalities increasingly appeared in uniform at regional contests—men of military age gradually disappeared to harsher callings, leaving their birds to wives and mothers who struggled to care for them until the men should return. Although in the upper and middle-class echelons of society birdkeeping had appealed to both sexes, possibly slightly more to the women, the fancy proper had always been almost exclusively male. Now, however, the women had a foot in the door, and after the war their tastes had to be considered.

The biggest change brought about by the war, however, was the replacement of the canary by the budgerigar in popularity. In the 1960s the budgie even succeeded in toppling the dog and cat from their time-honoured positions as Britain's favourite pets.

On the face of it it would have seemed that the canary, with its mixed seed diet, its greater life-span, and its 400-year history of domestication, would have adjusted better to the privations of wartime birdkeeping than the budgerigar, and to an extent this was true. Pet canaries accompanied their masters to the battlefields. One owned by a petty officer of HMS *Exeter*, for instance, was hatched and raised during the battle of the River Plate without getting a single feather ruffled by the action. General Montgomery, incidentally, was among the army élite whose baggage included not the legendary white horse for the victory parade, which travelled with his arch-enemy Rommel, but a cage of canaries.

Meanwhile on the George Cross island of Malta, pet owners sorrowfully forced themselves to 'liberate' their birds, conscious that they could not ask for bird seed to be airlifted in at the risk of human lives. Much the same thing occurred on the Channel Island of Guernsey when evacuation orders arrived, though some residents had to remain, and stubbornly managed to keep their birds going on an unnatural diet. In the grimmest period of the Channel Islands occupation, when human beings were struggling for a handful of millet to make bread, canaries were kept alive on ground-up swedes and carrots.

Even in England, by the mid-war period, the specialist press was printing 'recipes' to substitute for conventional foodstuffs. By 1942 canary seed on the London market was changing hands at £35 a cwt—or £700 a ton—and pet stores were offering to pay growers' rate for any reasonable quantity of backyard canary seed or millet. By 1944-45 the retail price of canary seed was to reach £1 ($2.50) per lb! Alternative food for cage birds included hedgerow seeds of various species, and, specifically for budgerigars, rice soaked in cold water for twenty-four hours, rubbed in a towel and dusted with oatmeal, or brown bread baked and then put through a grinder or mincer.

Yet the budgerigar came through these hard times a stronger species. Canaries and canary breeders were more numerous in 1939, but the canary fancy was stratified into various specialist breed societies, which did not necessarily agree among themselves. The Budgerigar Society, on the other hand, though smaller was more closely knit, and possibly its higher proportion of middle-class members could more readily see the point of following the recommendations made to them by correspondence from the Society. They were urged to engage in selective culling, to ensure that available food was diverted to maintaining the 'best of the bunch', birds with the potential to breed future champions. The regional as well as the national budgerigar societies acted as agencies for members in pooling the best of the remaining stocks. In a way not

G   97

matched by the canary clubs they looked to the future. As early as 1942 the Budgerigar Society was discussing schemes whereby members who had managed to keep aviaries through the war would supply members returning from the forces with potential stud founders at cost price or less.

True, wartime casualties from fright among budgerigars in blitzed areas did occur—the parrot family seems more prone to shock deaths than do finches. Among canary owners, stories circulated of hens who sat tight while owners extinguished incendiary bombs only a few inches away from their nests! But in the budgerigars' favour, in addition to the efforts of the societies, they were at this time mostly living as aviary birds or even caged as true sex pairs, giving a more even spread of the sexes than in the pet canary population, which consisted of singleton male songsters. Also, the budgerigars were home-bred, whereas many canaries came from overseas. In 1939 sales of canaries from one German city alone were estimated to be worth £9,000, while Britain's export trade in pet and show canaries was valued at £50,000 a year.

Although it was to Germany that roller breeders still looked for class in singing canary cocks, it was in Holland that the 'red factor' was developed. The red factor had first become feasible in the early 1930s, and many experts of the 1970s claim that progress towards a scarlet canary —nearly but not quite achieved with some of the latest red-factor types— was retarded twenty years by the total loss of the Dutch Leeuwarden strain when the Low Countries were occupied in the 1940s.

In England the 'London Fancy' was pronounced extinct in 1945, and the lovely lizards came perilously near the same fate. The total population of show-bench standard lizards was reduced to a mere ten individuals by the end of the war and all present-day lizards can be traced to this tiny force of survivors.

The United States, where work had progressed on both the development of Glosters and on the red factor during World War II, could have provided new blood. However, shortage of dollars prevented the average fancier from taking advantage of this pool and most British and Continental fanciers were forced to start from scratch after the war.

Patio birdcage of the 1960s

Other postwar difficulties, like acquiring wood and other building materials to set up aviaries in a country where house-building was the first priority, forced many returning soldiers to turn from canaries to budgerigars.

The show budgerigar of the postwar boom years was almost un-recognisably different not only from its wild ancestor but from the colony-bred budgerigar that had been kept as a 'moving feature' in the landscaped gardens of the upper middle classes between the wars. The result of 100 years of selective breeding, particularly from 1945 onwards, was a big bold-headed broad-chested specimen, which was available in more than sixty variations on the basic brilliant and pastel shades of blue, yellow, green, lilac, grey and white. Each of these colours, while subsequently developed and modified by fanciers, was the result of a natural mutation—a freak individual in fact. The budgerigar fancy believes that new colours occur about every five years.

The expert breeder's nightmare is that such a variation remain unrecognised in an amateur's aviary. Even less likely to be detected as of value by the amateur is the offspring of the new colour variation, which may, itself, have reverted to the colour of its 'ordinary'-colour grandparents. Such birds may, however, carry in their genetic makeup the ability to pass to their chicks the qualities of their new-colour parent. New budgerigar strains require not only to produce individuals that will so impress the show bench that they inspire fanciers to experiment with them, but a genetic heritage that enables them to be reproduced easily.

During the early 1950s the trend in show budgerigar production was towards the large bird, the ultimate being the 'long flight' variety with a beak-to-tail-tip length of 11 in or over. This bird was prized for a while by some fanciers as a breeding backstop against the danger that too great a concentration on a particular colour combination might result in undersized birds, but it had the disadvantage of being coarse-feathered, and since the subsequent ruling by the Budgerigar Society that the length of show specimens should be 8½ in overall, it has virtually disappeared from the scene.

Catering for budgerigars is now big business. To promote their packeted range of budgerigar foodstuffs the giant Petfoods Ltd set up in 1956 the Budgerigar Information Bureau, a public relations department designed to spread the gospel of budgerigar keeping wider than ever before. It was BIB that offered the £500 reward for the production of the legendary pink budgerigar—still, of course, to be claimed, since most breeders regard it as a genetic impossibility as well as an undesirable deviation from their present policy of refining and improving existing types in accordance with the Budgerigar Society's standards.

By 1959 the budgerigar population of Britain had reached 6 million, with an estimated 32,000 owner/breeders sufficiently interested in their

Shop display of budgerigars in Liverpool, 1969; fancy cages designed by the shop's display department

pets to join a budgerigar society. The apparently insatiable demand for budgerigars from 1955 onwards encouraged many experiments in breeding on a commercial scale. The BIB published a series of 'blueprints' showing that budgerigar studs could be set up for sums ranging from a few pounds to over £500, and set up its own model bird farm at Phipps Ford, Needham Market, Suffolk. This unit, then considered the world's biggest budgerigar-breeding establishment under one roof, consisted of 1,000 pairs of birds in sixteen units, breeding on the colony system and free to choose their own mates as they would in nature. It has subsequently been agreed, however, that no one can make a living from budgerigar breeding, or even make it a really profitable hobby, and by the 1970s the budgerigar population had fallen to a more realistic 2–3 million in Britain. Some of the breeders who once anticipated high profits failed to take into account that the birds live for seven or eight years, and despite the high toll of accidental deaths and escapes in the home, it would take about a decade for a nation's budgerigar population to need replacement.

The world of the budgerigar fancy and of the interested lay owner separated further during the boom years of 1950–65. Indeed, at the peak of the boom the fancy was even denied its traditional role of supplying would-be pet owners from its reject stock by commercial units geared not to producing the perfect show bird but directly to breeding healthy, lively birds suitable for the pet trade. The pet of this period was essentially a single bird, valued for its affectionate nature, its constant activity and, above all, its ability to mimic human speech. Although with dogs and cats the postwar demand has been for pedigree animals, this has not been so with cage birds, partly because the fancy is geared to a two-year turn-over of stock—with birds culled once their peak breeding efficiency is passed. They may sell birds that have failed to meet championship standards to less ambitious owners wanting them only as pets, but the public prefer to have baby birds straight from the nest. By the 1970s, with pressure from the commercial units, the average price fell to around £1.50 ($3.75) for a healthy young cock bird—a price at which no breeder could make a living.

Another reason for the decline of the budgerigar as a household pet in recent years has been greater family mobility. As more families have come to regard the weekend drive to coast or country—often with overnight stay in cottage or caravan—as customary, they have often given up pets that cannot be taken with them. A bird which has been caged alone all its life, and has come to rely for companionship on its owners, may well pine or show such signs of boredom as feather-plucking if abandoned for long periods, even when well supplied with food by a neighbour. This is perhaps why the budgerigar was supplanted by the tropical fish as the commonest pet at the end of the 1960s. In an effort to retain custom, bird-food as well as charitable organisations have developed schemes to distribute budgerigars to hospital patients, old-age pensioners and prison inmates, and indeed the therapeutic role of the cage bird is probably appreciated more today than ever before.

Certainly the bird world can proffer one spectacular example of this therapy. Confined to the island prison of Alcatraz for life, murderer Robert Stroud, better known as *The Birdman of Alcatraz*, became interested first in wild bird visitors to his cell and subsequently, when allowed to keep pet canaries, became not only a model prisoner but one of the world's leading authorities on these birds. His *Diseases of the Canary*, published in 1933, and his subsequent *Digest on the Diseases of Small Birds* are standard works in veterinary colleges dealing with small animals the world over.

In the United States there was a similar boom to Britain's in budgerigar breeding during the early 1950s. There, however, without the impetus to improve physical conformation of the war years in Britain, the concentration of the budgerigar fancy has tended to be almost wholly on the production of unusual colour. For good 'type' birds Britain remains the world centre. British stud budgerigars sell not only to the States but all over Europe. In Germany the cult of the budgie now seems likely to eclipse even the traditional pre-occupation with the canary. Budgerigar populations are also rising dramatically in Denmark and Holland, which now seem ripe to repeat the British experience—though both still draw their best bloodstock from British sources. Budgerigar populations are also high, and increasing, in Finland, Belgium, France and Switzerland, in that order; it is noticeable that each of these nations is becoming an ever more sophisticated and urbanised community.

Lord Snowdon's aviary at London Zoo

104

CHAPTER SIX

Pleasure Gardens and Zoos

Although at first it might seem that the car was the enemy of aviculture, since it takes the potential bird owner away from home for most of his spare time, and has reduced the keeping of domestic budgerigars, it has also caused a proliferation of pleasure gardens that seek to provide the family party with a day out—ideally in the open air and perhaps mixing amusement with 'education' for the children. We seem to have readopted that Victorian concept. The British tax system, forcing aristocratic owners of 'stately homes' to throw open their grounds and mansions to the visiting tripper at so much per head, has played its part. The most successful of these new professional entrepreneurs, such as the Marquis of Bath at Longleat and the Duke of Bedford at Woburn, have become skilled in a new kind of specialised entertainment. Their success has not only led to purely commercial ventures like the Windsor Safari Park, which is unrelated to a stately home and garden, but also caused long-established, scientifically biased zoos to improve their entertainment value for visitors.

In addition to these pioneers, a third group—landowners still wealthy enough not to have to ask the public for patronage, but who have always opened their grounds a few times a year for charity—have had to think of redesigning their aviaries, which are beginning to look out of date. A television-owning public, accustomed to seeing wildlife films, has become much more critical of the animal exhibits in these gardens, zoos or bird parks. It wants to see not just the canaries and budgies from any pet store or private home, but exotics—and, moreover, exotics housed in natural habitats, as far as possible. This changing attitude has brought about a spate of aviary construction, some of it in preserving historic aviaries and some in reproducing former aviaries in seventeenth, eighteenth and nineteenth century styles. There have also been new developments in aviary design—the most dramatic in the western world probably being the aviary designed by Lord Snowdon in association with Cedric Price and Frank Newby for the London zoo and completed in 1965. The London zoo had not been much in the news since the 1920s, when it improved its bird collection by introducing numerous exotics, and built a small bird house (in 1925) for a mixture of finches.

Lord Snowdon's brief was to provide quarters for Indian and African birds, including cliff-nesters, water birds, and ground, tree and shrub dwellers. The public were to be allowed to view the aviary from the outside and also to walk through it. The site selected was a difficult one, on the sloping bank of the Regents Canal, with a 22 ft drop from the top to the bottom. The aviary was described by the critic of the *Architectural Review* for September 1965 as 'one of the few large tensile structures in Britain in which the original design has not been coarsened'. Rather less flatteringly the building was also seen as 'a vision of collapsed goal posts among the trees', a sentiment shared by many of the residents of the expensive streets surrounding the Park, who felt the bucolic view for which they paid so dearly had been spoilt by the starkness of the structure —the first major work in this idiom since Powell & Moya's Skylon for the 1951 Festival of Britain on the South Bank of the Thames.

The aviary measures 150 ft by 63 ft, with its longer side parallel to the canal. The above-ground structure projects 20 ft at the ends and 13 ft at the sides, and rises 80 ft above the lower path. There is a 58 ft rise from the upper level of the aviary. Each of the sheer legs is 54 ft long by 2 ft in diameter. The aviary is made of aluminium mesh fabricated in 12 ft by

4 ft panels and connected with crimped aluminium. It is supported on tension cables anchored to the triangular aluminium end frames.

The eye-catching feature of the aviary is a 40 ft prestressed concrete cliff with waterfall effects. The plants, which extend beyond the aviary at both ends, were specially chosen to withstand nibbling by the birds. The suitability of the aviary for its job—despite its unconventional, and now dated, appearance—has been proved by the breeding records of the inmates and the delight of the visitors at being able to wander among them at two levels.

Since the construction of the 'North Aviary', as the Zoo still formally describes it, Lord Snowdon's taste in bird houses seems to have mellowed to the prettiness of eighteenth-century pastiche. Certainly the aviary he created for the Queen Mother's budgerigar flock is very like the unfulfilled design of the eighteenth-century landscape artist Humphrey Repton, which can be seen as a watercolour sketch in the Victoria & Albert Museum's print room in London. Both are hexagonal structures combining a bird display with a rose pergola, though Repton calls his 'an aviary in the Chinese manner' and Lord Snowdon calls his 'Romantic Gothic'. As mentioned earlier, the Snowdon design was marketed—at over £800 or around $2,000, with erection fees still to be covered by the purchaser—and sold well in both Britain and the United States.

The growth of aviaries as sidelines to 'garden centres' has been a recent feature of aviculture. One of the most impressive bird-flower combinations may be seen at the Springfields showgrounds of the Lincolnshire bulb growers; it is estimated to attract over 140,000 visitors during April and May. The attraction that the aviaries have for visitors has been much remarked, and some fancy pheasants have been added to the original budgerigars. Plant-selling 'garden centres' with bird displays find that while children gaze, parents will spend freely without harassment! Since these firms also sell young birds in season, to keep their own stock in check as well as to make the project pay for itself, they too are helping to revive the aviary as an expected feature of the attractively landscaped garden.

1971 birdcage table-lamp from the Derek Fowler Studio pottery

This feature has been notably used at the Syon House Garden Centre on the north bank of the Thames in Middlesex. The original intention was to create an aviary in eighteenth-century style to harmonise with the famous 'Great Conservatory' there, but the problem—one that besets many contemporary aviary builders—was how to compromise between the need for a highly decorative exterior and the welfare of the birds themselves. At Syon the latter interest won; but in Portugal Peter Coats separated the aviaries from the main part of the garden, and in their place has created a birdcage conceit—a large porcelain birdcage filled with brilliantly coloured china birds made to his direction by students of the Hammersmith College of Art. It is this setpiece that links the aviaries to the gardens proper.

Coats, incidentally, claims that his porcelain birdcage was partly inspired by the Fountain of Birds at the castle of Schwetzingen in Germany, which he featured lavishly in one of his illustrated books on the history of gardening. It was the work of Pigage, aided by the head gardener, Petrini, in the 1750s, and consists of water-spouting bird sculptures in a round pond surrounded by a circular trellis topped with bird statuary, the whole resembling a giant birdcage.

An aviary in the Indian style, popular in England around 1800, was added to Sezincote, a house at Moreton in the Marsh, Gloucestershire, about 1956, and now houses an impressive collection of budgerigars. Another recent reconstruction in the old-world style is the shell house-cum-dovecote introduced by Lord Boyd at Ince Castle, Cornwall. The shell house, designed by Lady Boyd, is of concrete blocks rendered in cement and sand, painted blue grey on the base and hung with local slates on the top. There is a wooden finial in the centre of the roof, and the design of the dovecote/shell house is continued in small decorative obelisks in the surrounding gardens.

Another example of the return of aviaries to the English garden can be seen at Heaselands, country home of Ernest Kleinwort at Haywards Heath, Sussex. Here, since 1968, an extensive parakeet-breeding project has flourished; it grew from small beginnings—an aviary housing a few budgerigars close to the swimming pool and patio section of the garden.

Peter Scott's sterling work with wildfowl at Slimbridge on the River Severn in Gloucestershire has inspired several similar establishments round Britain, such as the 23 acre Bentley Wildfowl Collection at Holland, Lewes, Sussex, and the Cricket St Thomas Wild Life Park, Chard, Somerset, where there is a system of lakes and waterfalls stretching for 3–4 miles. What of course makes Slimbridge so special is the way in which the resident population—many of which, like the Hawaiian geese raised here in the 1950s, can be used to replenish the numbers of an endangered species—is swelled by migratory visitors. During the spring of 1970, 1,200 young birds were raised at Slimbridge and 570 different species visited the sanctuary, consuming a ton of wheat and biscuit meal every four days. Subsidiary reserves are now in process of being established by this Wildfowl Trust in Norfolk and Scotland.

The Slimbridge Wildfowl Trust has been copied in locales as varied as Taiwan and the West Indies, and its offshoots still keep in touch with the parent trust. One example is the Pointe de Pierre Wildfowl Trust of Trinidad and Tobago, which regularly exchanges specimens with Slimbridge.

One trend in modern zoos and bird gardens is to give the inmates as much freedom as possible, and surprising successes have been achieved in acclimatising tropical types to temperate-zone weather. Free-flying parrots are one of the attractions of the Tropical Bird Gardens at Rode, near Bath for example; and Chester zoo claims to have one of the finest tropical houses in Britain—an area simulating equatorial forest—as well as a temperate bird house providing specially good accommodation for waterside species. Another trend in zoos is mixing congenial species of plants, fish, birds and even small mammals in a house maintained at a temperature and humidity similar to their natural habitat. It saves heating to mix several species, and it also gives visitors a better notion of how the flora and fauna would look in their natural surroundings.

A further development is the 'walk-through' display, where birds are contained only by areas of darkness round their enclosure through which they will not pass. This technique was first tried with humming birds, but has now been extended to other species. Indeed, once the technique has been perfected the 'cage-less' cage may well supplant the conventional birdcage in the home, birds being kept in artificially lit 'natural' environment 'tanks' set into alcoves.

In 1970 the facilities for visitors to the famous Harewood House, near Leeds, Yorkshire, were extended to include bird gardens. These are not, as at many 'stately homes', based on eighteenth or nineteenth century examples but are specifically designed to please the coach parties and family motorists of today. Covering four acres of gently sloping ground between the stables and the lake, they display over 200 species, with cranes and flamingoes at liberty and a modern-style tropical house. The penguin

The tropical house at Chester Zoo; the birds are free-flying, so not conspicuous

pool, of which the estate is especially proud, consists of two spring-fed ponds, the deeper with a glass front so that visitors can watch the penguins as they swim under water. Liberty macaws can be seen on the lawns in front of the house. Another recently created Yorkshire pleasure ground offers less attractively, a 'parrot circus': the birds 'play cards, roller skate, pull chariots, drive a car, ride a bicycle on a tight rope amongst other tricks'. Across the Pennines, the penguinarium of Belle Vue zoo, Manchester, is justly famous, as is the collection of flightless birds.

The world's largest assembly of pheasants is to be seen at the Norfolk Wild Life Park, Great Witchingham, Norfolk, the headquarters of the

Pheasant Trust, whose policy is to establish breeding groups of the rarer species and reintroduce them to their native habitats wherever necessary. Breeding here has been highly successful, no fewer than 284 birds of 41 species having been raised in one year recently, including—oddly for a pheasant trust—an impressive selection of young European owls.

American conservationists are similarly anxious to preserve the passenger pigeon, now extinct in the wild, in some kind of semi-captivity in the USA. The chough in Cornwall is another example; now virtually extinct

Turkish birdcage with overall decoration of mother-of-pearl, solid brass filling and hook on top. Designed for a small species, dating from approximately the turn of the century

this bird was once common enough to become the county's emblem, and a bird garden at Padstow is hoping to breed enough young birds eventually to restore some to the wild.

Conservation is of course the motive behind much modern aviculture. Now that the severe effects on wild bird populations of modern farming methods, including the destruction of habitats and the use of poisonous crop sprays, are more widely understood, the conservationists and the aviculturalists have been brought together, though in the past they have not always seen eye-to-eye. A problem that has arisen is that while many bird enthusiasts would be only too willing to supplement their bloodstock pools with an infusion of wildlings (which would be trapped), protective legislation in some countries, such as the British Protection of Birds Act, 1954, prevents this. In Britain, any native species publicly traded must bear a closed leg-ring of the type that can only be fixed within a few days of hatching, thus proving the bird to be captive-born. In fact conservationists would not object to such constructive, limited trapping—and indeed many bird enthusiasts now talk in conservationist terms themselves, considering the stock they hold as a 'national reserve' from which, if need be, the wild population could be replenished.

Many newer zoos have been founded with the preservation of wild life in mind, and many older zoos have added special collections of birds or animals in danger of extinction. Ireland's Dublin zoo, in Phoenix Park, can show a flock of over fifty flamingoes, and the largest waterfowl collection in Europe; Scotland's Edinburgh zoo has a flock of free-flying night herons which in 1970 raised fourteen young. Most North American zoos have extensive aviaries, the giant one at Detroit zoo being one of the main attractions.

In the emergent nations, the development of national parks for the tourist trade may do much to preserve African birds, and there are plenty to preserve. For example, in Kenya, Tanzania and Uganda, there are 1,300 species, compared to only 775 in the USA and 577 in Europe.

In Holland the concept of the pleasure park can be seen at the Avifauna Park, Alphen on Rhine, which gives sanctuary to a 100-strong stork

Modern steel-section aviary designed as the centrepiece at an exhibition, filled
with budgerigars

colony. The stork's habit of returning to its northern nesting grounds in springtime has made it in Nordic folk lore the bringer of all young life—including human babies—and it would be a pity if this charming legend were to die. Avifauna Park also has extensive and attractive wader pools and tropical houses, designed in local architectural style, in parkland settings, complete with typical Dutch windmills in miniature. One of Europe's most splendid private aviaries is in the villa of Dr Eugenio and Dr Pietro Callegari at Ravenna in Italy, where birds are housed on a scale that must be the envy of many zoos. The Callegaris have been particularly successful in breeding grebe in captivity. These birds are housed in splendid quarters—an aviary 40 ft long by 15 ft wide and 8 ft high has an 18 ft pool, continuously fed with spring water to keep it crystal clear. The whole area is attractively planted.

Sophia Loren's Villa Ponti, just outside Rome, has extensive aviaries sited well away from the house, and masked by flowers and shrubs in such a manner that only the colourful flight patterns of the birds themselves, and not the design of the aviaries, catch the eye. Another delightful Roman aviary can be seen in the garden of the Villa Lante. Its double dome is typical of the sixteenth and seventeenth century Italian style, and in fact the villa's owner, Dottore Cantone, had it copied from a seventeenth-century birdcage, which is now preserved in the nearby orangery. At Cleres in France, too, impressive breeding records have been achieved in the grounds of an old château.

In the Orient, aviculture has throughout history taken its own pattern. In Hong-Kong, for instance, where the closely crowded conditions make the keeping of any but the smallest pets an impossibility, the Chinese appreciation of nature makes birdkeeping a favourite pastime for rich and poor. Most Chinese fanciers, again because of the problems of housing, do not breed their own birds but rely on the regular trapping of wild ones. Favourite species are the Chinese zosterops, green singing finches, and various species of lark. The usual diet given to singing softbills is ground soya-bean meal, supplemented by maggots, lizards and insects. Live lizards as bird food are a regular part of market trading in the city

Contemporary German birdcage

116

and command a steady sale despite the comparatively high price, in relation to wages, of about 3p or 7–8 cents.

Singing birds compete with each other, their owners wagering large sums in the special bird cafes and teahouses. These places provide hooks where owners can hang their cages while they refresh themselves, and over the years have virtually developed into birdkeeping clubs. Fighting birds are also kept—usually magpies, robins or black-faced laughing thrushes. The prelude to a fight is for the cages of the contestants to be placed alongside each other. The contestants then square up for a sing-off as part of their natural behaviour. Should one cock fail to meet this verbal challenge, obviously his owner loses the bet, but if both sing freely then they are placed in a single cage to fight. The sparring is not, as with the old English cock-fight, to the death, but merely lasts until one bird has gained the upper hand; since the birds are extremely valuable to their owners, it is usual for the loser to call off well before his bird risks serious injury. Since the prime condition of the birds is also a source of pride, they will only be fought two or three times during a 'season'—only in the spring is the fighting instinct sufficiently strong to make a contest relatively certain.

Chinese cage with elaborate silver chasing

CHAPTER SEVEN

The Cage-Collecting Craze

The antiques boom since World War II has priced the traditionally collectable articles, such as eighteenth-century silver or old pottery, out of the average European collector's range, so dealers have had to find other items for him to collect. Such items have had to be small, for postwar homes, and decorative. It was also necessary that they should illustrate the craft skills of other days, and say something about the day-to-day life of their former owners. On all these counts the antique birdcage was an obvious winner.

The earliest birdcages likely to turn up in shop or saleroom will probably be seventeenth-century Dutch, designed for the canaries or singing finches then popular. Baroque in style, many of these cages may well utilise precious materials such as ebony or ivory in their construction. Tiered shapes on a circular base, becoming narrower toward the top, are typical of this period, though some of the simpler specimens—mainly those intended for suspension—are bell-shaped. Small finials in turned ivory are common, and blown glass is a favourite material for the food and water vessels.

As would be expected, a cage is much more valuable if it still has all its original fittings. Seventeenth-century Dutch cages were often intended to have silken tassels or glass lustres pendant from the base, and it is not unusual for a round cage to be set into a square wooden base. Utrecht Museum in Holland has some excellent specimens. Another seventeenth-century variety sought out by collectors is the large domed curled-wire cage still widely made and exported from Tunisia and the North African coast generally. It almost certainly came to Europe in the wake of the Moorish invaders, as did the all-ceramic decorative birdcages. Both types are still manufactured in Spain, and are popular tourist souvenirs as well as being exported via Spanish handicraft shops such as the Casa Pupo chain. This chain also carries some traditional hand-crafted cages in wrought iron suitable for terrace or patio, or for indoors, prices being around £60 or $150.

The ceramic and wire cage designs were taken to the Low Countries when these were Spanish provinces, and were also directly imported by Dutch traders during the sixteenth and seventeenth centuries. In Dutch cities famous for their pottery, such as Delft, the Moorish porcelain bird-cage was adapted to the local blue-and-white chinaware style, and once again a continuous tradition of manufacture runs through to the present day, making the accurate dating of cages of this type extremely difficult.

Birds, caged or not, were in fact popular motifs of the famous Dutch tile industry from the seventeenth century on. Both blue-and-white and full-colour tiles were made in the industry's heyday, about 1750. Parrots in bell-shaped cages are a favourite pattern. Tiles showing bright yellow canaries in aubergine-coloured wire cages have recently appeared on the London market and have been sold for around £10 each. Although rich materials may be used for the seventeenth-century cage, its form will tend to be simple and the lines pleasingly functional.

By the eighteenth century, fantasy was beginning to creep in. By now caged birds were fashionable with the rich, and their taste, in contrast to that of the solid burgher of the previous century, encouraged the production of much more delicate-looking cages. With France setting the pace in interior decoration and garden planning, openwork gilt-wire cages came into fashion about 1700 and remained popular throughout the eighteenth

Parrot on coloured tiles

121

century. They are best shown in the casing of the singing automata popular in the late eighteenth and early nineteenth centuries.

There were also a number of experiments with birdcages in the eighteenth century, but these—like the frail contemporary wire cages, and the lantern-shaped rush cages still favoured by the poorer bird fancier—have not survived their own times. Consequently, the collector is more likely to find a sturdy seventeenth-century cage than a failer cage from the following century.

An exception to this rule is the doll's-house cage, which began to appear in the 1730s, often as a copy of a Palladian-style country mansion. The design continued to be used until the end of the nineteenth century, by then copying the red-brick suburban villas of the Victorian middle class,

Eighteenth-century 'dolls' house' birdcage

122

and becoming a favourite in the nursery. Some of the cages survive because they are mainly made of wood; often the barred section is at the ends, the front depicting the facade of a house, and the back remaining plain so that the cage could hang or stand against a wall. Quite often the 'windows' are fully glazed and some cages even boast the interior fittings of a house, with perches acting as miniature 'minstrels' galleries'. Almost invariably such cages are quite large 'one-offs' made to order by a local carpenter, and oblong in shape.

They are nearly always speedily snapped up in the sale room because of their charm and novelty; prices range from £80 ($200) for late Victorian specimens to £200 ($500) for the rarer eighteenth-century models. They can be dated by their style of architecture. The country-house sale is a good place to find them, though sale-room catalogues may not list them as birdcages: the last cage of this type to pass through Christie's sale rooms in London was listed under dolls' houses. Wire cages, however, are catalogued under ephemera or household furniture, according to their size.

Some dolls'-house birdcages were also made in Germany. They are smaller than British models, and of course illustrate German architecture, with its steeply angled roofs and dormer windows. Tiny decorative wooden cages were also made in Germany, in the eighteenth century and particularly in the early nineteenth, when the export trade in German roller canaries was at its peak. These come both in wire and as box cages with solid backs, the latter being the more common. The box cage favours the pediment and pediment-shaped curves over the wire front, and all sorts of gilt work. Gingerbreaded and fretted wood-carving, involving cable-like twists of wood, swags of simulated drapery, urns, spirals and flourishes are typical of the fancy cages of the Harz mountain regions. The double-headed eagle, with or without the companion motif of crossed flags, is also frequently employed in the design of German cages of the 1820s.

Some German cages are barrel-shaped, but the usual form is oblong, about 50 cm high, with flat and narrow sides. The feeder pots of the early Dutch cages in washable china or glass often revolved for refilling, but the

German pots pull out like drawers, and the food containers themselves are made of wood. Sometimes they form projections like miniature 'side chapels'.

These small German cages remained popular with the poorer bird fancier as show cages. They continued an eighteenth-century approach to decoration, such as miniature classical columns, baroque gilt work and similar trimmings, while cages for the rich patron dropped these embellishments.

Bell-shaped brass parrot cages began to appear around 1780 all over Europe, and they can be dated by their cylindrical feeder pots. These cages were simple and elegant, the only decoration often being a cut-out metal panel round the base. From the 1750s, however, cages for small birds began to reflect the diverse influences of the period: chinoiserie vied with mock Gothic.

The use of mahogany and rosewood marks the Regency in England. Before this period, and slightly into it, Continental birdcage designers used golden-tinted woods, often with marquetry panels in contrasting colours, for by now the large free-standing indoor aviary was a cabinet-maker's piece, often ordered to match a set of furniture.

On the European Continent the combination birdcage and jardinière was popular in column shape. These pieces are very much sought after on the market; they are usually in better condition than the smaller bird-cages of the same period—a good specimen recently changed hands in London for the record figure of £975 ($2,440). It was made of inlaid fruitwood, and 5 ft tall with a lead-lined flower pot at the top, and brass wire throughout. It could have been used straight away, though in general it is not wise or humane to use antique birdcages for living birds. The original inhabitants were canaries or goldfinches.

Small table birdcages of the period 1800 to 1830 would now fetch £80 to £100. The fashion for oriental styles provoked a number of minaret-like cage designs or pagoda-like structures in which red lacquers were used

Regency-style birdcage with lift-off top

to add to the effect. Also around this period a metallic decoration similar to today's ric-rac braid (gimp) seems to have become popular, often in a contrasting shade to the rest of the cage. It was quite common, too, for the door to be a fake or only semi-functional at this time; for getting inside the cage, the roof, which was secured by a metal clip, was lifted off.

Although not yet factory-produced, cages by the early nineteenth century, when the lower middle and working classes took up birdkeeping, were made to a formula, and the collector will come across several of the same type. Many have rusted badly and are in need of more loving renovation than better-quality earlier specimens. Bars may well have to be soldered back into place and the whole repainted before the cage is fit to be exhibited, but its value will be increased by restoration.

In the 1820s the basic bell-shape of ceramic birdcages began to grow a base ledge, giving the cage the appearance of sitting on a cake stand. This style had been made from the 1780s onwards, but it became much more widespread from the 1820s, and remained a favourite parlour cage for the English market for the next thirty years. The cake-stand base was taken up by factory producers of metal cages, and is, in fact, to be seen in many of the designs taken from contemporary trade catalogues that illustrate Shirley Hibberd's *Rustic Adornments for the Home of Taste*. Here the idea of windows cut into solid side-panels persists in the designs of cages intended to house siskins or grass parakeets.

The cake-stand base is also retained in the Zollverein patent cage, a combined canary cage and goldfish bowl in the 1850s. The fish bowl is surmounted by a crown-like structure, and the birdcage itself is shaped like an outwardly curving pillar with sloping roof. The whole is based on a scalloped dish with faceted stand. The Zollverein looks top-heavy, and is an example of ornament spoiling function.

One of the eyecatching exhibits at the 1851 Great Exhibition at the Crystal Palace, London, was a birdcage constructed of blown-glass rods, set on a tasselled blue velvet cushion, itself presented on a polished wood

Blown-glass cage, 1851

126

tray. It won its inventor a prize, though it was not intended to house live birds, just to be decorative.

The nineteenth-century love of ornamentation inspired the production of a number of birdcages in which even the Victorians and their Continental contemporaries hesitated to confine birds. These are in fact products of the model-makers' art, such as the spired 'Gothic cathedral' birdcage, one of the most prominent exhibits in the Vogelbauer Museum, Neheim Husten, twenty-five miles east of Dortmund, in Germany. This is to date the world's only museum devoted to birdcages and birdkeeping equipment. Privately owned and within the plant of the Voss birdcage-manufacturing company, which produces 400,000 cages a year, it was set up in 1945. Joseph Voss, head of the firm, first began collecting antique birdcages for his own amusement, after a seventeenth-century wooden cage had caught his eye in a Dutch antique shop. He was able to buy the item for a mere 300 marks, to discover subsequently that a similar cage was one of the star exhibits in an Amsterdam museum.

Today Voss has over eighty birdcages on permanent view, and a further thirty are lent to department stores and other bodies for display at exhibitions, etc. The museum also houses a fine collection of prints, photographs and books on the history of birdkeeping; and its curator, Norbert Hamburg, has published an authoritative and lavishly illustrated manual on the collection. The museum takes most pride in its Durer engravings, though the 15,000 visitors who pass through it yearly take more interest in the do-it-yourself and professional manuals on cage-making, which date from 1600. Two of the most interesting exhibits are a reconstruction of a cagemaker's workshop and an itinerant salesman's barrow from the canary-raising districts of the Harz mountains.

The 15,000 sq ft of permanent exhibition in the museum include birdcages from Sweden, Switzerland, Italy, France and Britain. The largest item is a re-creation of a Roman birdcage—originally part of the set of a period film—which was rescued by Mr Voss from a Munich

'Gothic Cathedral' birdcage

I

junkyard. Among the modern cages is a South American wickerwork model of Mexico City cathedral, complete with spires and clock. There is also a comprehensive selection of Swedish and German 'chalet type' peasant birdcages in carved and painted wood and wire, dating from the 1850s.

Twentieth-century cages are of course less interesting than older ones. After 1914 the gilded-wire cage gave way to chrome—the smart medium of the 1920s. A matt finish took over in the late 1920s and 1930s but super-sheen chromes returned after World War II when, during the budgerigar boom, there was also a fashion for cages with horizontal bars. These were supposed to be 'kinder' to the climbing instincts of the budgerigar, though most breeders would contest this, claiming that encouraging the budgie to climb about its cage made the risk of damage to flight and tail feathers the greater. The fashion for companion budgerigars during the 1950s encouraged the production of drop-fronted 'play cages', which could well become curios of the future. Free-standing horizontally barred cylindrical cages enjoyed a brief run in the 1950s, but these were surely the worst-designed cages since the eighteenth-century dolls' houses, imposing a helicopter-like motion instead of the normal horizontal flight on the poor birds. Some collectors enjoy seeking out the small, cheap cages that can be found overseas. The Hong Kong bird fanciers, for example, often use cages of unvarnished split bamboo with wooden bases, though even these will usually boast food and water vessels in fine hand-painted china. The rich owner often possesses a cage made of precious metals, with ivory perches and blackwood bases inlaid with mother of pearl. It is not unusual to find the feeding vessels carved from solid jade.

By European standards, most Chinese birdcages are much too small actually to house birds, as are those domed cages in curled wire now frequently seen in European or American homes as souvenirs of holidays in Spain or North Africa (Tunisia in particular). Such cages, and also the

Bamboo cage, after Mexico City cathedral

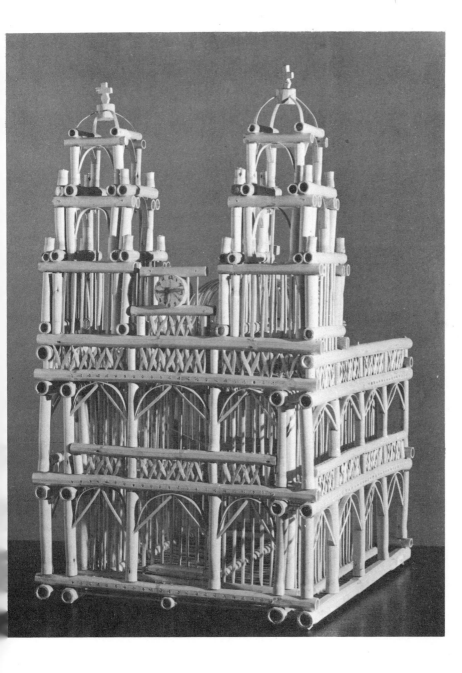

elaborate woven rush or bamboo South American cages that sometimes turn up in handicraft or antique shops, are only suitable as ornaments.

In the western world, cage design has been remarkably static in modern times. Plastics are used for side panels and feeding pots in small cages, and fibreglass for wader pools and rock formations in large aviaries, and for the small domestic aviary rigid acrylic plastics and lightweight metals, but attempts at modern design for the ordinary owner have been something of a failure. For example, when the magazine *Cage Birds* ran a readers' competition for the design of new and interesting pet-bird

The 'Crystal Palace' cage, 1960s

housing, the bulk of the extensive entry merely re-used the prettier shapes of the Victorian era.

To encourage the keeping of budgerigars in aviaries the British Budgerigar Information Bureau has several times organised outdoor cage-design competitions, and sponsored manufacturers who have designed sensible but attractive cages—such as the bureau's own pitch-roof cage for the terrace. The BIB and the Budgerigar Society would much prefer cages to be bigger than at present, but according to the pet trade, customers will not pay enough. Thus large cages of the 1950s and 1960s like the Crystal Palace and the Arundel, which were designed primarily for looks rather than price, have now been dropped from production, and that could make them collectors' pieces of the future. The Crystal Palace was made by the century-old firm of Charles Palmer Ltd, and had a domed roof that had to be finished by hand like Victorian birdcages.

At the luxury level, stores such as Harrod's and Heal's, London, can sell aviaries in cedarwood or white wire for the patio at £45 ($112) or so, faster than their suppliers can turn them out. A few cylindrical aviaries on wheels, with painted metal canopies, have also been imported now and again, at about £60 ($150). But the luxury market looks to the past for its designs, and modern prefabricated cages in such materials as stainless steel or aluminium have mostly been commercial failures, although a modern aviary was one of the centrepieces of an exhibition of antique and exotic birdcages at the London Tea Centre in the 1960s. Several 'gingerbread'-work German cages of the late eighteenth and early nineteenth centuries were on view, as well as a delightful Turkish barrel-shaped cage inlaid with mother-of-pearl. Intended for a small singing finch, it had undoubtedly been originally designed as a seraglio ornament.

A display of interesting and exotic birdcages of past and present, along with living birds, is to be seen at a 'stately home' near Lewes, Sussex. In the former stable wing of Glynde House can be seen some of the small wooden cages once belonging to working men of the eighteenth and nineteenth centuries, the type on which modern show cages are still

Arundel cage, 1960s

134

largely based. These cages can still occasionally be picked up for a matter of pence in junk shops and on market stalls, though even here the demand is overtaking the supply, since they are frequently used as plant containers. Antique birdcages have indeed been a favourite gimmick of professional interior designers. Antique ceramic cages have also been used, as at Glynde, as lamp bases or even lamp shades.

Bird pictures and porcelains are also worth collecting today. The best-known pictures of all are of course those of Audubon's *Birds of America*, copies fetching vast prices in the London or New York sale rooms from time to time, and modern reproductions of them also fetching big sums. Also well known are the porcelain bird statuettes of the late Dorothy Doughty, and the Boehm series of bird sculptures in china clay, made at studios near Malvern, England, as well as in the USA. These cost anything from around £70 ($175) to nearly £2,000 ($5,000) when new, and as they are produced in limited numbers only will appreciate in value. The price sounds less excessive when it is remembered that the 43 inch model of the mute swan, introduced in 1970, needed 8 tons of plaster of paris for the moulds from which the 151 sections for each model were cut, and that each specimen requires the most intricately skilled painting.

Some interesting eighteenth-century prints of bird-sellers and aviary designs are to be seen in the Victoria & Albert Museum in London, but in general the birdcage has not been considered worthy of specialist study. So there is ample scope for the private collector to become an expert, studying and assembling pictures and books, even if he cannot afford or house many cages. The really interesting old cages do not often come under the hammer, though any specimens acquired would make a sound investment.

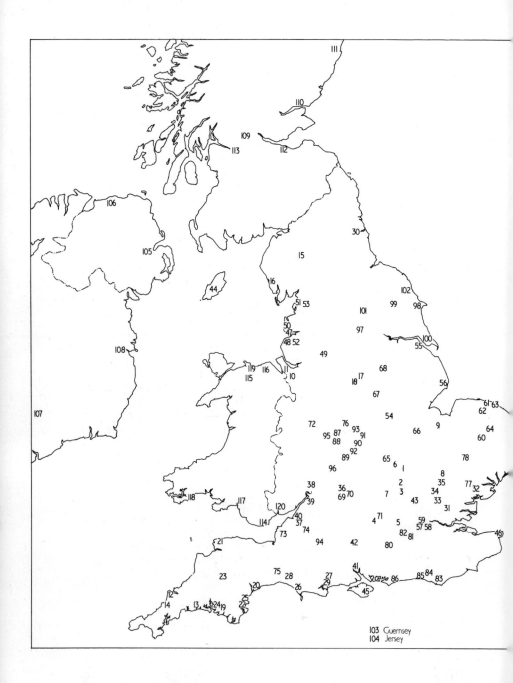

111

110

109 113 112

106

105

30

15

16 102 99 98

44 51 53 101 97 100 55

50 49 68 56 61 63

47 18 17 67 62

48 52 54 64 60

108 119 116 11 10 72 76 93 91 66 9 78

115 95 87 88 90 92 89 65 6 8 35 77 32

96 1 2 34 33 31

107 118 117 38 36 70 7 3 43

120 39 69 59 57 58

114 40 37 74 4 71 5 82 81 46

73 94 42 80

21 41

23 75 28 27 29 20 a 86 85 84 83

12 20 26 45

14 13 24 19 25 22

103 Guernsey
104 Jersey

County-by-County guide to 120 establishments of interest to birdlovers

BEDFORDSHIRE
1 Stagsden Bird Gardens, Stagsden.
2 Woburn Abbey, Woburn.
3 Zoo Park, Whipsnade, Dunstable.

BERKSHIRE
4 Child-Beale Trust, Exford Road, Pangbourne.
5 Safari Zoo, St. Leonard's, Windsor.

BUCKINGHAMSHIRE
6 Flamingo Gardens & Tropical Bird Zoo, Weston Underwood, Olney.
7 Waddesdon Manor, Waddesdon, nr Aylesbury.

CAMBRIDGESHIRE
8 Linton Zoological Gardens, Mortimer House, Linton.
9 Thorney Wildlife Park, Thorney, Wisbech.

CHESHIRE
10 North of England Zoological Gardens, Chester.
11 Woodhey Bird Farm, Haddon Lane, Ness, Neston, Wirral.

CORNWALL
12 Bird Gardens, Fentonluna Lane, Padstow.
13 Murrayton Wildlife Sanctuary, St Martin-by-Looe.
14 Trenance Park Zoo, Newquay.

CUMBERLAND
15 Lowther Castle Wildlife Park, Penrith.
16 Muncaster Castle Bird Garden, Ravenglass.

DERBYSHIRE
17 Ashover Zoological Gardens, nr Chesterfield.
18 Riber Castle Fauna Reserve and Wildlife Park, Matlock.

DEVON
19 Dartmoor Wild Life Park, Sparkwell, nr Plympton, Plymouth.
20 Exmouth Zoo, Exmouth.
21 Ilfracombe Zoo Park, Comyn Hill, Ilfracombe.
22 Paignton Zoo & Botanical Gardens, Paignton.
23 Pinevalley Wildlife Park, Okehampton.
24 Plymouth Zoo, Central Park, Plymouth.
25 Teignmouth Children's Zoo, Shaldon, nr Teignmouth.

DORSET
26 Abbotsbury Swannery, Abbotsbury, Weymouth.
27 Merley Bird Gardens, Wimborne.
28 Park Wildfowl Farm, Broadwindsor.
29 Poole Park Children's Zoo, Poole.

DURHAM
30 Stanley Zoo, Harperley Hall, Tantobie, Newcastle-on-Tyne.

ESSEX
31 Brentwood Miniature Zoo, Coxtie Green Road, Brentwood.
32 Colchester Zoo, Stanway Hall, Colchester.
33 Harlow Children's Zoo, Harlow.
34 Wildlife Park, Stansted.
35 Mole Hall Wild Life Park, Mole Hall, Widdington, nr Newport.

GLOUCESTERSHIRE
36 Birdland Zoo Gardens, Bourton-on-the-Water.
37 Bristol Zoo, Clifton.
38 Falconry Centre, Newent.
39 Wildfowl Trust, New Grounds, Slimbridge.
40 Wildlife Park, Westbury-on-Trym, Bristol.

HAMPSHIRE
41 Southampton Zoological Gardens, The Common, Southampton.
42 Weyhill Zoo, nr Andover.

HERTFORDSHIRE
43 Verulamium British Wild Life Zoo, St Albans.

ISLE OF MAN
44 Curragh's Wildlife Park, Ballaugh.

ISLE OF WIGHT
45 Isle of Wight Zoo, Sandown.

KENT
46 Safari Wild Animal Park, Dreamland, Margate.

LANCASHIRE
47 Birdland and Aquarium, St Anne's Pier, Lytham St Annes.

48 Birdville, Marine Parade, Southport
49 Zoological Gardens, Belle Vue, Manchester 12.
50 Blackpool Zoo and Aquarium, Tower, Blackpool.
51 Marineland, Morecambe and Heysham.
52 Southport Zoo, Princes Park, Southport.
53 Winged World, New Heysham Head, Morecambe.

LEICESTERSHIRE
54 Lion Reserve, Stapleford Hall, Melton Mowbray.

LINCOLNSHIRE
55 Marineland & Zoo Ltd, Humberston, Cleethorpes.
56 Skegness Natureland, North Parade, The Promenade, Skegness.

LONDON
57 Battersea Park Children's Zoo, SW11.
58 Crystal Palace Children's Zoo, Anerley Hill, SE19.
59 Zoological Society of London, Regent's Park, NW1.

NORFOLK
60 Banham Zoo, Grove Farm, Attleborough
61 Cromer Zoo, Howard's Hill, Cromer.
62 Kelling Park Aviaries, Kelling Pines, Holt.
63 Nature Park, Cromer.
64 Norfolk Wildlife Park and Ornamental Pheasant Trust, Great Witchingham, nr Norwich.

NORTHAMPTONSHIRE

65 Coton Manor Wildlife Garden, Guilsborough, Northampton.
66 Wildfowl Trust, Waterfowl Gardens, Peakirk, nr Peterborough.

NOTTINGHAMSHIRE

67 Sherwood Zoo, Broomhill Park, Hucknall.
68 Sundown Pets Gardens, Treswell Road, Frampton, nr Retford.

OXFORDSHIRE

69 Carterton Bird Gardens, Brize Norton Road, Carterton.
70 Cotswold Wildlife Park, Bradwell Grove, nr Burford.
71 Wellplace Bird Farm, Ipsden.

SHROPSHIRE

72 Pets Corner, Weston Park, Shifnal

SOMERSET

73 Ambleside Water Gardens and Aviaries, Lower Weare, Axbridge.
74 Tropical Bird Gardens, Rode, nr Bath.
75 Wildlife Park, Cricket St Thomas, Chard.

STAFFORDSHIRE

76 Drayton Manor Park & Zoo, Fazeley, nr Tamworth.

SUFFOLK

77 Daws Hall Wildfowl Farm, Lamarsh, Bures.
78 Norton Petsenta, Norton, Bury St Edmunds.
79 Suffolk Wildlife and Country Park, Grove Farm, Kessingland, Lowestoft.

SURREY

80 Birdworld, Holt Pound, Farnham.
81 Chessington Zoo, Burnt Stub, Chessington.
82 Egham Woolly Monkey Sanctuary and Bird Garden, Great Fosters, Egham.

SUSSEX

83 Drusillas, Berwick nr Alfriston.
84 Bentley Wildfowl Collection, Holland, Lewes.
85 Brighton Aquarium & Dolphinarium, Marine Parade, and Madeira Drive, Brighton.
86 Children's Zoo, Hotham Park, Bognor Regis.

WARWICKSHIRE

87 Birmingham Botanical & Horticultural Society Ltd., Westbourne Road, Edgbaston, Birmingham 15.
88 Birmingham Zoo, Cannonhill Park, Pershore Road, Birmingham 29.
89 Charlotte Pheasantry, Charlcote, nr Warwick.
90 Coventry Zoo Park, Whitley Common, Coventry.
91 Nuneaton Zoological Gardens, Plough Hill Road, Chapel End, Nuneaton.
92 Southern Zoo Farm, Southam, nr Leamington.
93 Zoo Park, Norton-juxta-Twycross, nr Atherstone.

WILTSHIRE

94 Lions of Longleat, Longleat, Warminster.

WORCESTERSHIRE

95 Dudley Zoo, Castle Hill, Dudley.

96 Delamere Bird Gardens and Aquarium, Hill Furze, Fladbury, Evesham.

YORKSHIRE
97 Bird Gardens, Harewood House, nr Leeds.
98 Sewerby Park Zoo, Bridlington.
99 Flamingo Park, Kirby Misperton, nr Malton.
100 Burton Constable Hall Bird Gardens, Sproatley, nr Hull.
101 Knaresborough Zoological Gardens, Conyngham Park, Knaresborough.
102 Scarborough Zoo, Scarborough.

CHANNEL ISLANDS
103 Children's Zoo, La Villiaze, St Andrews, Guernsey.
104 Wild Life Preservation Trust, Les Augres Manor, Jersey.

NORTHERN IRELAND
105 Bellevue Zoological Garden, Belfast.
106 Benvarden Lion Park, Co Antrim.

EIRE
107 Falconry of Ireland, Clonmel, Co Tipperary.

108 Royal Zoological Society of Ireland, Phoenix Park, Dublin 8.

SCOTLAND
109 Blair Drummond Safari Park, nr Stirling.
110 Camperdown Children's Zoo, Dundee.
111 North of Scotland Zoo, Hazlehead Park, Aberdeen.
112 Royal Zoological Society of Scotland, Edinburgh 12.
113 Zoological Society of Glasgow, Calder Park, Glasgow.

WALES
114 Cardiff Zoo, Weycock Road, nr Barry, Glamorganshire.
115 Gwydir Castle, nr Llanrwst, Denbighshire.
116 Llannerch Zoo Park, St Asaph, N. Wales.
117 Penscynor Bird Gardens, Cilfrew, Neath, Glamorganshire.
118 St Catherine's Island Zoo, Tenby
119 Welsh Mountain Zoo, Flagstaff Gardens, Colwyn Bay, N. Wales.
120 Whitsun Zoo, Whitson Court, nr Newport, Monmouthshire.

Index